THREE HOUSES

To My Father and Mother

[Mackail]

Angela ↓Thirkell, 1890-1961

THREE HOUSES

Robin Clark Ltd

First published in paperback in 1986 by Robin Clark Ltd
A member of the Namara Group
27/29 Goodge Street
London W1P 1FD

Originally published in Great Britain by the
Oxford University Press, 1931
Fifth impression, 1947
Morley Baker Edition, 1970
Copyright © Angela Thirkell

British Library Cataloguing in Publication Data

Thirkell, Angela
    Three houses.
    1. Thirkell, Angela——Biography 2. Novelists,
    English——20th century——Biography
    I. Title
    823'.912   PR6039.H43Z/

    ISBN 0-86072-103-5

Reproduced printed and bound in Great Britain

Introduction

RICHARDSON'S GROTTO

IN the summer of 1751 Samuel Richardson invited a party of friends to his country house at North End to hear a reading of the manuscript of *Sir Charles Grandison* in the grotto. His guests were Mr. Mulso, Mr. Edward Mulso, Mr. Highmore, Miss Mulso afterwards Mrs. Chapone, Miss Prescott afterwards Mrs. Mulso, Mr. Duncombe a clergyman, and Miss Highmore, who afterwards married Mr. Duncombe. Mr. Highmore had been engaged on a portrait of Mr. Richardson, and Miss Highmore who was also something of an artist made a drawing of the company seated in the grotto. It is a bare plastered room with a stone floor, a few steps below the level of the garden, looking out on to a pleasant vista of gravel path and waving poplars. Mr. Richardson in a brown turban and wrapper is seated with his legs crossed (an attitude which the young artist found it a little difficult to reproduce in a convincing way), reading aloud. The gentlemen are sitting in various elegant and unstudied attitudes, a hand thrust into the waistcoat or waving approval. The ladies in black gowns and white kerchiefs, with black shady hats over their white caps, cluster round a table on the right. Miss Highmore herself is occupied with what looks like a book and a pencil, as if in the act of transferring Mr. Richardson's venerated features to paper.

Miss Highmore, writing later to Miss Mulso, said, 'I should think that you did my rude sketch too much honour by preserving it and taking it with you, were it not for the respectable persons attempted to be represented.' Luckily the future Mrs. Chapone valued the rude sketch, and when in 1804 Mrs. Anna Laetitia Barbauld made her selections from Richardson's correspondence in six volumes, Richard Phillips, the publisher, had it reproduced in colour as a frontispiece to the second volume.

North End Lane was far out of London then, the best part of a mile beyond the gates of Holland House and well on the road to Richmond and Twickenham, but the female admirers and their swains came undauntedly in their heavy coaches to taste the delights of tea-drinking and literary conversation with the kindly old man, so susceptible to their flattery. Johnson, we know, wrote of him as 'an author who has enlarged the knowledge of human nature and taught the passions to move at the command of virtue'; but it is difficult now to think of Richardson in these terms and we see him rather as Henry Esmond Warrington saw him at Tunbridge Wells, 'the immortal, little, kind, honest man with the round paunch', a bevy of admiring ladies surrounding him.

Richardson died in 1761 and his world departed. But the house with the grotto remained, the mulberry tree in the garden grew and spread, and more than a hundred years after his death a poet and a painter, walking on a Sunday afternoon by fields and lanes from Kensington, saw it and were strongly attracted by it as it stood tenantless. The poet was William Allingham, now better known through the black-and-white illustration that Rossetti made for his poem, 'The Maids of Elfenmere'. The painter was Edward Burne-Jones. My grandfather was then looking for a house where he could live and paint, and The Grange, in spite of early nineteenth-century alterations and a layer of stucco over the old red-brick front, was full of charm and possessed one large room on the first floor which could be made into a studio. So in 1867 he and my grandmother went to live there and for thirty years the house was filled with hopes, work, love, and the constant intercourse of many friends.

The original twin houses were built by Justice Smith in 1713–14. About 1836 they came to be known as The Grange, the name which the north house has kept. Richardson took the north house on lease in 1739 and *Pamela, Clarissa Harlowe,* and *Sir Charles Grandison* were all written there. The Grange passed through various hands and in 1863 the houses were inhabited by the fourth Marquis of Londonderry who threw them into one, making several structural alterations. In 1867 when my grandparents went to live there the two houses were again separated, but the north house had lost some of its original character and its handsome square staircase had been replaced by a long flight of stairs opposite the front door against the party wall. It is not known exactly when the front was stuccoed over but it was probably in the early years of the nineteenth century. At the same time the dignified sash windows at the front of the house were reduced in number and clumsily altered. The south house is still in its original state and is by far the more handsome as it is the larger of the two. North End Lane was a shabby enough thoroughfare at its northern end, but as one walked down it the little houses and shops soon came to an end and there were prosperous, comely, red-brick houses of Queen Anne's time, each standing in its own garden with fields behind. To-day these fields and gardens are covered with mean houses or ugly pretentious flats and genteelism has re-named the district West Kensington, but the words, 'The Grange, North End Lane, Fulham', take me back to the eighteen-nineties and summers of miraculous length and warmth when it was always Sunday and one played for endless hours in a sunny garden.

Part One

THE GRANGE

I SUPPOSE every one has a mental picture of the days of the week, some seeing them as a circle, some as an endless line, and others again, for all I know, as cubes and triangles. Mine is a wavy line proceeding to infinity, dipping to Wednesday which is the colour of old silver dark with polishing and rising again to a pale gold Sunday. This day has a feeling in my picture of warmth and light breezes and sunshine and afternoons that stretch to eternity and mornings full of far-off bells. How varying are the evocations of bells. They have almost as much power to startle a memory to life as the odours which annihilate the years between us and our childhood. Wherever I am in the world, a grey warm Sunday with the sound of bells coming damped through quiet unceasing rain will mean Oxford to me. In the underworld, twelve thousand miles away, that sound of bells in steady rain has translated me for a moment to Oxford in early summer and the scented drip from hawthorn and laburnum. And even now to hear bells in London on a June morning makes me lose the many intervening years and go back to a pale gold Sunday when the sun shone on an endless leisured day.

Long ago—say thirty-five years ago—a little girl used to wake on Sunday morning feeling that a whole life of happiness lay before her in the day. She had a low bed in her mother's room and her mother had a four-post bed with thick curtains patterned with birds. If it was not too early and her

mother was awake she was allowed to get into the big bed
and have conversations till the dressing gong rang and the
smell of sausages began to rise from the kitchen. Sunday
sausages: what a world of emotion in the words. Sacred
Sunday Sausages, I had almost said. There can be no other
dish which so obviously fits the day, especially with bread
fried in the same pan. Some are fat and burst in the middle;
others have a little twist at the end which we called the night-
cap; but all are divine.

What a pleasant leisurely meal was Sunday breakfast.
There was no motor to be propitiated and all one's friends
were in town and could be visited later in the day, so breakfast could go slowly from sausages to scones and butter and
honey, and then to strawberries and cherries. The little
girl's mother would read aloud afterwards while we all sat
at the table and pushing aside cups and plates drew pictures
out of whatever book was being read. During a reading of
Burnt Njal one of the children drew an imaginary portrait
of Skarphedinn and he was used to mark the places in all
our Sunday morning books till 'Skarphedinn' became
synonymous with 'bookmarker' in the family.

So breakfast took its leisurely course till eleven o'clock or
so when we had to go upstairs and be cleaned and dressed
for Sunday lunch with our grandparents. Perhaps the golden
haze is needed when we come to Sunday clothes, for they
were a little inhuman compared with the freedom of to-day.
My brother may have been let off comparatively lightly with
blue blouse and knickerbockers, a holland smock, brown
shoes and socks, and a sailor hat whose elastic was always
too tight or too loose; but for me there was the ordeal of

Starch. Buttonholes starched so stiffly together that one couldn't force the buttons into them; starched petticoats which were rather fun to put on because they crackled so as you pulled the folds apart, but had complications of starched tapes at the neck which needed Nanny's relentless fingers; white piqué frocks with full sleeves standing up like crinolines and all the hooks ironed flat so that Nanny had to lever them open with the nursery nail-scissors; white pinafores with frills round the neck; white cotton gloves, well stiffened, into which one's hot hands were with difficulty thrust; black shoes and long stockings and then the straw hat with a wreath of flowers and the inevitable elastic. How it hurt when it was half an inch too short and how inelegant it looked when Nanny had tied a knot in the middle to shorten it.

At last we were ready and set out with our father and mother for North End Lane, Fulham. All that neighbourhood is genteel now and the street is called North End Road, West Kensington, but while this golden Sunday lasts we need not think of changes. We went up Young Street from Kensington Square, past the old shops at the corner, past John Barker's little drapery establishment, and got into a red horse bus opposite the church. Six on each side inside and fourteen outside—how small it sounds now. The table of fares, hand-painted, with its convention of a wiggly line connecting stopping-places and fares did not hold more than a dozen names. On we went, past the old brick houses standing back on both sides of the road then, past the leafage of Holland Park, past more terraces of old houses and over the railway bridge. No buses went down North End Lane and we walked along past early eighteenth-century houses, each in its own garden of elms and cedars and mulberries. The air was warm, the sun shone on the blossoming trees hanging over the brick walls, and so we came to The Grange.

The Grange stood a little back from the road behind a brick wall with an iron gate in it. A short flagged path led to the low front door. It had a glazed upper half and green silk curtains to prevent people looking in, but people of the right size could always look through the letter-box. The low square hall must once have been a front parlour, but it had been thrown into the passage and made a pleasant room to play in, heated in winter by a large green earthenware stove called Pither. At its further end were the stairs and a long passage leading to the drawing-room and the door to the kitchen quarters.

On Sunday my grandparents kept open house. Two or three extra places were laid at lunch for any friends who might drop in, but whoever came, I sat next to my grandfather. I was allowed to blow into the froth of his beer 'to make a bird's nest', or to have all the delicious outside from the mashed potatoes when they had been browned in the oven. If, disregarding truth, I said that at home my toast was always buttered on both sides, my statement was gravely accepted and the toast buttered accordingly. There can have been few granddaughters who were so systematically spoiled as I was and it is a legend that the only serious difference of opinion which ever arose between Gladstone and Burne-Jones was as to which of them spoiled an adored grandchild the more.

The Grange

After lunch my grandfather often settled down to a game of draughts, which was a good moment for my brother and myself to escape and do a little exploring upstairs. My grandparents surprisingly clung to the Victorian convention of a drugget, and though a thick-piled Morris carpet was on the stairs I do not remember ever seeing it without its cover. At the top of the staircase was a long landing with rooms opening off it, but just in front of us three broad shallow steps went up to the studio. Their banisters curled outwards at the bottom and a child could squeeze comfortably behind them and be in a little house. At the top of these steps a window on the right looked out over the large garden next door. Here too was kept a kind of gigantic tin bath on wheels, painted red, filled with water in case of fire.

It was a lucky day if we were able to slip into the studio which was as a rule absolutely forbidden. Sinister people called 'models' lived there who had trays taken up to them at lunch and tea-time. There was a strange smell of oil and turpentine. It was very easy to lose things. My necklace or pencil, once rashly pushed through the grating in the floor where the hot-water pipes lived, was irrecoverable. Even more rashly one might push one's belongings through one of those mysterious S-shaped holes by which the studio seats and stands were picked up and carried about. This done, they would rattle about till doomsday, like the silver eggspoon which my brother put down the hole of the rocking-horse's pommel, and nothing would get them out. Then there were gloomy corners fenced off by canvases where at any moment one might bring an easel clattering down on one's head or upset a little china pipkin full of some precious mixture. As long as I can remember there was a studio man who stoked the furnace, did odd jobs, and kept the brushes and palettes clean. The first studio man we knew was called William, because his name was so impossibly Albert. He had been in South Africa and I remember crying with rage when he confessed, under severe cross-examination, that the Kaffir children were more like my brother's shoes which were dull black than like mine which were patent leather. He was replaced in time by Pendry, a strange dwarfish creature who could play the Jew's harp with exquisite skill and imitate Punch, and convulsed the nursery by pretending to fall down with fright at the dragons on a Chinese rug.

Beyond the big studio was an inner room, down a few steps, a place of great danger to us, for here lived the lay-figure, its arms and legs at preposterous angles, its papier mâché head perched rakishly on its long neck. By daylight we jeered at it and it was known as 'Silly', but we had some dread of its possible powers by night. From this room a door led to my grandmother's sitting-room, but it was never used. It was in this sitting-room, papered with the Pomegranate pattern on a dark blue ground, that I had my only remembered sight of William Morris of whom, although he was such an old friend and so often at the house, we children saw but little. It is entirely unworthy of notice except for the peculiar circumstances which imprinted it on my memory. I was trying to read a book which I had laid on the carpet, while my body and legs were on the sofa and my elbows on the floor. This attitude of extreme discomfort appears to have been necessary to make me notice the old man (or so I thought him), with the aggressive mop of white hair who was talking, between fits of coughing, to my grandmother.

Having succeeded in visiting the studio unseen, it was just as well to slip away again before our absence was noticed, so we decided to give the kitchen the pleasure of our company and ran downstairs and along the back part of the hall. Here under the stairs lived another red fire-bath—I really don't know what else to call it—and yards of neatly coiled canvas hose which I am sure no one would have known how to use if there had been any danger. On the other side of the hall was the service hatch to the kitchen, but looking through it we found that the inhabitants were still sitting at dinner, so we judged it better to keep away for the present. At this point there was a choice of pleasures. We could go into the drawingroom and so through the French windows to the garden, or take the long passage with the skylight. This route had the advantage of avoiding the grown-ups who would probably want to stop one doing what one wanted, or make one do something one didn't want to do, so we went quickly down the passage past the filter. The long narrow storecupboard on the left was unfortunately kept locked, or we might have put in some good work among the currants and lump sugar. The garden, full of sunshine, gleamed alluringly through the open door at the end of the passage, and out we ran.

As soon as we were out of the house we might have been in the country. Gardens surrounded us on all sides and only a few years earlier there had been fields behind the little orchard which bounded the further end. Ugly brick houses had been built since then, but they were hidden by the long white rough-cast studio which stood between the orchard and the road. It was called the Garden Studio, and here my grandfather worked on his larger canvases. It was a little alarming to us: the red-tiled entrance and steps which led down to the furnace-room where we were never allowed to go and anything, one felt, might live; the iron grills in the floor to let in the warm air for winter days; the tall narrow slit in the outer wall through which finished pictures were passed. Sometimes these pictures went to exhibitions, but more often straight to the friend or patron (in the very best sense of the word) who had commissioned them and was content to wait for years if need be for the perfect expression of the artist's mind. In this studio there was a very high set of steps with a higher and lower platform on which the artist worked at the upper portions of his picture. I remember sitting on these steps, my head wrapped in a many-coloured piece of silk and bound with a coronet, while my grandfather made studies of crown and drapery for one of the mourning queens in the great unfinished picture of Arthur in Avalon which is now in the Tate Gallery. Here too he was working at the time of his death on the picture —also unfinished—of the Car of Love, now at South Kensington, where Love, standing in a great brazen chariot, is drawn through the thundering streets of some imagined city by a throng of his worshippers, some happy, some stabbed with pain, but all his slaves.

Because there is a certain likeness between the little girl who wore the coronet and some of her grandfather's pictures, she has often been asked whether she sat to him.

The Grange

As far as I remember he never used me as a model except on that one occasion when I wore the crown and veil. Nor in any case could he have drawn me often, as I was not yet eight years old when he died. Neither did my mother who was pure 'Burne-Jones type' sit to him much. The curious thing is—and it ought to open a fresh field of inquiry into heredity—that the type which my grandfather evolved for himself was transmitted to some of his descendants. In his earlier pictures there is a reflection of my grandmother in large-eyed women of normal, or almost low stature, as against the excessively long-limbed women of his later style. But the hair of these early women is not hers, it is the hair of Rossetti's women, the masses of thick wavy hair which we knew in 'Aunt Janey', the beautiful Mrs. William Morris. When I remember her, Aunt Janey's hair was nearly white, but there were still the same masses of it, waving from head to tip. To any one who knew her, Rossetti's pictures—with the exception of his later exaggerated types—were absolutely true. The large deep-set eyes, the full lips, the curved throat, the overshadowing hair, were all there. Even in her old age she looked like a queen as she moved about the house in long white draperies, her hands in a white muff, crowned by her glorious hair.

But when my grandfather began to develop in a different direction from his master Gabriel he saw in his mind a type of woman who was to him the ultimate expression of beauty. Whenever he saw a woman who approached his vision he used her, whether model or friend. Some of my grandparents' lasting friendships were begun in chance encounters with a 'Burne-Jones face' which my grandfather had to find a way of knowing. As my mother grew up she was the off-spring of her father's vision and the imprint of this vision has lasted to a later generation. I do not know of another case in which the artist's ideal has taken such visible shape as in my mother. If the inheritance were more common one would have to be far more careful in choosing one's artist forbears. El Greco, for instance, or Rowlandson, would be responsible for such disastrous progeny from the point of view of looks.

From the Garden Studio we might have been tempted to make a forbidden excursion into the street, but the outer door was locked so back we ran into the little orchard. Small enough it was, but large enough to a child, with space to sling a hammock from pear-tree to apple-tree and a green bench for grown-ups and a bank to roll down. In those days soot had not choked the blossom and there were plenty of windfalls in autumn for us to eat when Nanny's eye was not on us. On the other side of the orchard was a little shrubbery where the gardener kept his tools and had a huge rubbish heap and grew a few pot-herbs. The place was memorable to me because I once in a fit of unwonted zeal weeded up a whole bed of spring onions. The gardener did not approve of our presence here, so we went round by the great flowering elder-tree and came back on to the lawn behind the house. Here, against the south wall, was an immemorial mulberry-tree, its spreading boughs supported by posts and the cracks in its ancient bark plastered with cement. After the fashion of mulberry-trees it was good to climb and good to stain one's pinafore. Near it, also against the wall, was a little grassy mound known as Pillicock Hill. You will remember

The Grange

Edgar's song in King Lear, 'Pillicock sat on Pillicock-hill', and there was a nursery rhyme,

> Pillicock sat on Pillicock's hill.
> If he's not gone he lives there still.

Sometimes on my brother's birthday my grandmother had a Punch and Judy show on the lawn, as much for our grandfather's pleasure as for ours. He had the highest admiration for Punch and said of him: 'I really do think Punch is the noblest play in the whole world. He's such a fine character, so cheerful, he's such a poet, he chirrups and sings whole operas that are not yet written down, till the world bursts in upon him in the shape of domestic life and the neighbours.' There was also a legend that my grandmother had once given a garden party with the Blue Hungarian band, but that was so unlike all we knew of our grandparents that we accepted the tale with utmost caution. The only circumstance that we knew in any way paralleling it was when some ladies and gentlemen came on a winter afternoon to see pictures and we were sent for to the drawing-room after tea. The big room was dimly lit, its Dürers and Mantegnas barely visible, and seeing strangers I felt it incumbent on me as hostess to welcome them by flinging my arms round their necks. One of the ladies knelt down and let me hug her properly, but the tall gentleman was very stiff and though I tugged at his hand he wouldn't bend. It wasn't till much later that our scandalized Nanny informed us that the kneeling lady was called Alexandra and was a princess. The tall stiff gentleman was Prince Charles of Denmark then, the King of Norway now.

Three Houses

On the grass, among the pear-trees and apple-trees, we played for endless hours while people came and went with jingling and clip-clopping of hansoms between The Grange and other hospitable houses. The men played bowls on the lawn and smoked and talked and the women paced the gravel walk by the long flower-bed or joined them under the trees. Though we had been at The Grange for immemorial space, there was always time for further pleasures in those days when it was always afternoon. We might be put into a hansom and taken to other gardens with studios in them where our parents would talk and pace the paths and we would play among rose-trees and apple-trees and the very sooty creeping ivy peculiar to London gardens. All through the long afternoons the gardens waited for us. Draycott Lodge, where the Holman Hunts lived, Beavor Lodge and the Richmonds, The Vale, home of the De Morgans—all bricks and mortar now. Melbury Road, even then only a ghost of its old self where the Prinseps used to have their friends in a yet more golden age and where Watts still lived. Grove End Road, with Tadema's stories which were so difficult to understand until his own infectious laugh warned you that he had reached the point, the agate window and the brazen stairs. Hampstead, Chelsea, Hammersmith, gardens were waiting for us everywhere and people who made noble pictures and were constant friends.

At last the long afternoon came to an end. A final visit to the kitchen regions to talk to Robert the parrot and examine the hatch for the hundredth time and the hansom was at the door. Then a drive home in the cool of the day and the little girl was allowed to sit up to supper in her dressing-gown and have baked potato with a great deal of butter till she was half asleep and was carried upstairs in her father's arms while he sang—very slowly, so that the nursery should not be reached before the song was ended:

> My grandfather died, I cannot tell you how,
> He left me six horses to gang with the plough . . .

One more long happy Sunday had joined the pale golden Sundays that are gone. Better—to us at any rate—than Sundays now. Though these latter-day Sundays may be real enough, to us they are but the illusion and the bygone days the reality. There is always in our minds the hope that we may find again those golden unhastening days and wake up and dream.

Part Two

NEXT TO THE GREYHOUND

IT is not every one who has the luck to be brought up next door to a public house. When my parents were first married they went to live at 27 Young Street, Kensington Square, beside the Greyhound. The little house is still there and so is the public house; but it is not the Greyhound of my very young days. Then it was almost a country inn, a James II house like ours, two stories high with dormer windows in the high tiled roof, a front door in the middle and a window on each side. A small porch was built out over the front door and on its roof were two stone greyhounds couchant. It was at the 'Greyhound Tavern over against my Lady Castlewood's house in Kensington Square' that Esmond spent a wakeful night before the meeting at the King's Arms. Thackeray's own old house was opposite us and our landlady was Lady Ritchie who had been Miss Thackeray. Her son had been called Denis after his grandfather's Denis Duval and my parents called their son Denis for the same reason.

Old Kensington when I knew it was a vanishing dream, but how pleasant, how romantic it was. In an old inhabitant of the Royal Borough there is a secret nostalgia for its red-brick houses, its lanes that are now streets, its hawthorn flowering gardens that are flats and garages, its little friendly shops that were long ago swallowed up by great department stores. There is hardly a street in Kensington that has not been changed even in my lifetime. Part of Kensington

Square remains untouched, but the hideous tide of commerce is sweeping down upon it. On Campden Hill the great houses and gardens are falling one by one. Kensington Terrace, with its long gardens went many years ago. Scarsdale House was gone before I can remember. When first my parents went to Young Street they could look across gardens at the back of the house to the elms of Kensington Gardens. Flats cover those open spaces now and number 27 with its neighbour Felday House is left, a little island of green among high walls and overlooking windows.

When I came back to London this winter after many years' absence I found Lord Holland's statue gone from the green enclosure at the bottom of Holland Park, the old brick wall and railings pulled down, a great block of shops and flats in their place. Farther up the High Street, Phillimore Terrace was being carted away—the 'Dishclout Terrace' of George III—and the row of houses next to it where we used to run up and down the steps was gone. Even in Kensington Gardens I found the destroyer at work, asphalting tracks that were once like country footpaths, piling up bricks and mortar at the end of the Broad Walk and near the Round Pond, daring to alter the railings and borders of the Flower Walk, making germ-nests of sand in organized playgrounds where no self-respecting Nanny will let her children play. Farther afield they are setting up unnecessary monuments, some ugly, some merely common, or giving the green grass to be trodden into mud by football players so that twenty-two boys may enjoy themselves where hundreds could stroll or sit. I cannot see that any of these changes are for the better, but the great aim of democracy is to make everything as uncomfortable as possible for the greatest number, so the minority may hold its tongue.

I have only to turn my eyes into my mind and there I find the Old Kensington of my youth. It is a bright summer morning with the sun pouring into the panelled night nursery where I and my brother sleep in our iron cribs with Nanny between us. One can put one's head between the black enamelled bars, but it is not always easy to withdraw it. On the mantelpiece is one of those enchanting glass bottles containing a view of the Needles in coloured sand. Between the night and day nurseries is the interesting place where the water always came through in the winter. A regular accompaniment of wet weather in those days was the drip, drip of rain through the roof into a tin bath placed below it, for the house was a sad example of jerry-building, not unknown even in the days of James II. The walls were loosely filled in with rubble which had sunk lower and lower, leaving hollow passages for the rats and mice, while the lead on the flat roof of the night nursery was always in need of repairs. As for the bursting of water-pipes that was inevitable. Winters must be much milder now, or water-pipes of stronger constitution. Then it was accepted as a law of destiny that a pipe should freeze and burst at least once in every winter and there was the excitement of streams of water pouring down inside or outside the house and the nursery bath had to be supplemented with jugs and basins. It was at crises like these that the public-house next door could be so kind and helpful in bearing a hand till the workmen came. Or there was the fatal day when my father squashed a finger in the window and my mother being young and inexperienced fled shrieking to the Greyhound, who rallied at once and sent round to lift the window sash, rescue my father, and give first aid.

Our day nursery looked out on to the street. In winter the window was kept tightly shut and sausages of red baize filled with sand were laid along the openings to exclude the death-dealing fresh air. If it was freezing and the panes were covered with fronds and leaves and stars, Nanny would put a saucer of milk out for us overnight on the window sill. Next morning we would be allowed to eat the smutty congealed mixture. Our nursery ailments seemed to last for weeks then. Even a cold in the head was treated with infinite precaution and had its unchanging ritual. After several days in bed with a fire by day and an oil-lamp by night, we were allowed one afternoon to sit up to tea in a dressing-gown, near the nursery fire. Next day we were dressed, but confined to the nursery. On the following day we had our heads thickly muffled in shawls and were carried down to the drawing-room for a change of air. Next day, if it were fine, we were taken for a short walk between twelve and one, a scarf wound round our mouths and noses and such an outfit of woollen spencers, thick coats, woollen gloves, fur caps, gaiters, and boots, that we could hardly move. After this our convalescence proceeded on the usual lines.

Just opposite us lived a family of about our ages, and when we were all shut up in our respective nurseries with colds, we used to communicate across the street by breathing on the pane and writing a message backwards. A lengthy business—but time had no value then. Both nurseries liked to watch the lamplighter. When the early darkness had fallen we would lift a corner of the window curtain to watch for his coming and an answering gleam of light would come from the other side of the road, till the Nannies called us away from the draught and both curtains fell again.

There were times when winter fogs descended on London and the nursery was imprisoned for days together. Sometimes the fog was thick and yellow and choking, so that we could not see the messages on the pane. On more than one occasion there was the excitement of improvising beds for guests who had come to dinner and were fog-bound. Traffic was entirely held up where the fog was thick. A few brave four-wheelers went crawling along by the kerb. Little boys—descendants of those link-boys that used to thrust their torches into the iron extinguishers of the Kensington Square houses—sprang out of nothing and went about with lights, offering to see people home. The streets were curiously quiet except for distant cries from the High Street where a few carts and buses were trying to get to their homes.

At other times there was a terrifying black fog which lay like a thick cloud in the upper air, turning noon to midnight, while the air below was comparatively clear. Then the street rang with shouts and yells and the slipping of hoofs on stones and the grinding of brakes as the traffic, caught unawares without lights, crashed into narrow Young Street from both ends, John Barker's stables just beyond the Greyhound adding to the confusion, till the lamplighter, hastily summoned, brought his glowing pole and order was restored.

Next to the Greyhound

At such times my brother and I believed that great power was given to a mythical being called Mr. Ponting (no connexion of the draper of that name), who lived in the coal-cellar. Clasped in each other's arms we used to repeat his name, like an invocation of an evil spirit, till we had hypnotized ourselves into a state as near hysteria as one might wish. Mr. Ponting specially favoured fogs and never manifested himself at any other time.

In spring our nursery window was as good as a dress circle seat for seeing what went on in the square. On the first of May Jack-in-the-Green still came in his bower, accompanied by chimney sweeps dressed in gay colours who danced in the street for the pennies we threw down. On the same day all John Barker's horse-vans were drawn up in the Square before starting on their rounds, each horse with its tail and mane intricately plaited and bound up in ribbons and bright rosettes. Wherever we were on May Day we met charming horses all bedizened and gay, up and down the streets of Kensington. Then there were a number of itinerant musicians whom we knew by sight. The Highlander, with his Highland lass in tartans, playing the bagpipes, the girl frightening my brother dreadfully by picking him up and kissing him. The weekly German band, very clean and respectable, in uniform and peaked caps, each man with his little piece of music in a clip at the end of his instrument. The Italian organ-grinder with a monkey, in a red jacket and a little cap with a feather, who would take your penny and put it in his pouch. The man who was a walking orchestra; he had a hat covered with bells, a drum behind him which he beat with his elbows, strings attached to his

33

feet with which he twitched cymbals, pan pipes strapped under his chin, and his hands free for five or six other instruments. The Frenchman who brought a mild bear called Joséphine walking on her hind legs, ready for buns or fruit which she managed to eat through her muzzle. These and many more were our spring entertainers.

In summer the striped sun awning was pulled down and the green window-box filled with pink geraniums and musk. Nursery tea was delicious on these hot afternoons. We would come in hot and dirty from the Square and stump upstairs. The nursery window was wide open, the afternoon sun was tempered by the blue and white awning, the scent of the newly watered flowers in the window-box came in on the light summer breeze. Outside, a watering cart was being filled from a tall red pipe which curved over a hole in the top of the tank. When the water had slopped over the top the driver would turn the red pipe round so that it did not project over the road and mounting his seat, press the pedal which released the water through the holes at the back and go off leaving little blobs of water running about, dust-coated, on the dusty road. The nursery table was ready laid, only waiting for Nanny to boil the kettle in the dressing-room next door. We were not promoted to drinking tea yet. For us there were long refreshing draughts of milk from enormous flowered cups. I once bit a large piece out of one of them in my haste and the subsequent rivets were held up as an everlasting reproach to me. The butter was usually beginning to melt. It must have been at a cooler season of the year that I ate a half-pound pat whole while Nanny's back was turned. There were sometimes shrimps or potted meat or water-cress. Mustard and cress we grew ourselves in the garden, or on damp flannel, so that it tasted like sucking the bath sponge.

In those halcyon days of the Civil Service my father, who was in the Education Department, as it was then called, used to get back in time for tea. When he left the house in the morning he used to tell us that he was going to earn the bread and ask us what kind of bread we would like, white or brown. According to our answer he would bring us back a white roll or a Hovis loaf at tea-time. If things had gone very well he earned enough to afford to buy shortbread, but this was not so often. His bedroom was at the top of the house, an attic room that ran from back to front. It was a treat for me to climb the steep stairs that twisted round the great newel post which stood the whole height of the house from the basement to the top landing and visit him while he shaved. In this attic he wrote his life of William Morris, in the morning before going to work, or in the evening when we were asleep. As soon as we were tucked up in bed he used to come to the night-nursery and tell us the story of the Wooden Horse of Troy and the Wanderings of Ulysses. These story-tellings went on until, as we got older, our bedtime was too near the grown-ups' dinner for them to be squeezed in.

Sometimes I slept in my mother's room, where there were doves who were allowed to fly about the room. A couple of asses if ever I saw any! The gentleman dove spent all his time bowing and cooing to himself in the looking-glass on the dressing table, while the lady dove, neglecting the nest we had so neatly stuffed with artificial moss and hay, laid all her eggs from the perch on to the floor where such as did not smash at once were trodden underfoot by Mr. Dove when he came home in his hobnailed boots. Their passion for hairpins and bits of string may have been a primeval stirring towards making a nest, but it never got any farther.

One occupation I can thoroughly recommend if your heartless parents send you to bed while it is still light. You lick your finger and rub it up and down on the Morris wallpaper. Presently the paper begins to come off in rolls and you can do this till you have removed so much of the pattern that your mother notices it. Then you have to stop. Another excellent way of diversifying the monotony is to cry till your mother comes. I became an adept at working up a wholly fictitious grief till I was really sobbing. If Nanny was upstairs she came banging across the landing and told me to be quiet, but I was able to judge when she had gone down to the kitchen for her supper and then my wails increased in volume till my mother came tearing up from the drawing-room below to see what the matter was. By this means I had a quarter of an hour of her agreeable company and then, much refreshed, went to sleep. Her bedroom was only divided from the Greyhound by a party wall. On Saturday nights I could hear the singing next door quite clearly. The only song I remember was of a moral nature:

> Time is money and money is time,
> And don't you be forgetting it.
> Always get as much money as you can,
> And don't forget the time for getting it.

We were very lucky in having parents who could tell us

stories. My father not only told us all about Greece and
Rome, but he sometimes had a serial story of adventure
going on at the same time. It had a medieval spaciousness
and vagueness and once begun could go on for ever, or stop
without in any way affecting the plot. My mother also had
a story without an end about a brother and sister. This she
used to tell us after lunch while she was resting on the
drawing-room sofa. Drawing-room life goes on far above
the heads of people who are playing on the floor, so that
when Millais came to tea and we were sent for to shake hands,
I merely reported next day that I had seen the new doctor.
People would come and play something very dull called
Bach on my mother's harpsichord, and when Mr. Dolmetsch
came to tune it and told me to sing a scale I didn't know
what a scale was; but it seemed quite an easy thing to sing.

Before they went to The Grange, my grandparents had
lived at 41 Kensington Square, and we still had friends there.
At No. 40 lived my mother's godmother Lady Simon.
Every year on the third of June she used to send a huge
double birthday cake for my mother and brother whose
birthday was on the same day. Occasionally I was taken
in state to see her. She was a rather alarming old lady with a
very frank tongue, and though she was never anything but
kind to me, I was, for no particular reason, afraid to go
upstairs. I planted myself firmly on the doormat, saying in a
tearful voice, 'No thanky you—no thanky you', till my
mother had to give way and take me home. Farther along
was Edward Clifford who so astonishingly united a deep
and active feeling of religion, a passion for duchesses, and a
marvellous gift of water-colour painting. His daily work

was for the Church Army to which he gave time and devotion, shrinking from nothing in the early days when roughs made organized attacks on its meetings. But at home he was surrounded by lovely pictures and china and carpets and always had his drawing-room full of flowers from some great lady's garden. To us children he was kindness itself. It was one of our treats to visit him in his drawing-room and see his albums. He did what we should all like to do, mean to do, but somehow don't do: kept everything that amused or interested him, whether a joke from *Punch*, a bit of poetry from the *Westminster Gazette*, a coloured reproduction from a publisher's advertisement, an engraving of a bird or landscape, and pasted them all into huge albums. Among the miscellaneous cuttings were the most exquisite water-colour drawings done by him at one or other of the country houses where he stayed. My first art purchase was one of those drawings with which I fell madly in love—a field and trees almost black in the fading light, a house barely adumbrated with a glimmer in one window, above them a sky of palest green deepening to darkest blue above and one star shining. He let the little girl buy this at a nominal price with her savings and then gave her another—a fiery red afterglow reflected in pools of water. On another occasion when the little girl came to see him he asked what she would like for a present. Her swift and unhesitating answer was 'A knob'. Later on Mr. Clifford gave her a lump of chased silver with a hole in it, the head I should think of an old cane, and she was perfectly satisfied with her knob.

Another of the charms of his drawing-room was prisms of all shapes and sizes which dangled in one of the long windows. Sometimes we were allowed to wrench one off and take it with us and then we walked happily home, passing it from hand to hand, seeing the familiar objects fringed with red and yellow and violet. There was always preserved pineapple at Mr. Clifford's house, and while we ate it we strolled round looking at pictures. He had a peculiar gift for copying Burne-Jones' paintings so that my grandfather himself could hardly tell the difference. Two in particular I remember in his drawingroom, Merlin and Nimue, and Green Summer, both indistinguishable from the originals. He lived with a very tall friend whom we knew simply as 'the giant'. Clifford is dead now, with his funny affected voice, his strange mixture of romantic snobbism and religion, his kindness and capacity for friendship. I do not know who has the old house, but the giant's sister lived, not so many years ago, in a house on the south side of the Square, opposite.

Almost next to Mr. Clifford lived Vernon Lushington, a very early friend of my grandfather's. When the old Greyhound was cruelly pulled down and rebuilt as a commonplace gin palace, the two headless stone greyhounds were bought by the Lushingtons and put one on each side of their front door. The little Maid of Honour cottages just across the road from the Lushingtons have been pulled down after sinking to sad depths of dirt and neglect, and I suppose the old house with its snowy pear-tree will soon be sacrificed for the convenience of one of the big shops. Women have much to answer for. When I look at the idle jostling crowd of females (of which I am myself a part), which makes Kensington High Street impassable between eleven and five, I feel that my charming sex is perhaps at the back of all the destruction of Old Kensington. Lovely houses and gardens have had to go so that women may come up from Ealing and Hammersmith and Fulham and across from Notting Hill and Bayswater to 'look at the shops'.

On the west side of the square a white house with bright window-boxes was the home of Mrs. Patrick Campbell. My parents and grandparents loved and admired her, and to us she was 'Auntie Stella'. My father had made a special translation of *Pelléas et Mélisande* for her. We were all much in and out of each other's houses then. She would descend upon Young Street with a swish of silk and a froth and fluff of lace demanding nursery tea, or suddenly require a bed in a darkened room as it was impossible for her to rest in her own house. Sometimes I was sent for to keep her company in the curtained room. She dressed her little Stella, who was not much older than I, like a fairy princess, and I used to inherit pinafores made of the finest silk woven with gold and frocks of shimmering stuffs.

Going to her house was always an adventure because you never knew who was there or what might happen. Auntie Stella might receive me in bed with curtains drawn, lamentably moaning that she was an old woman and would never be nice to look at again. Or she might be trailing about the house in a long-tailed lace wrapper alternately scolding and caressing whoever came within reach, lavishing affection on Pinky Ponky Poo, her adored dog, companion for many years. One might find Mr. Yeats upstairs and M. Henri Bernstein downstairs while, neglecting them both, Auntie Stella might insist on taking me for a drive in a hansom and reciting *Mélisande* in French—she was going to act with

Sarah Bernhardt—begging her most incompetent companion to criticize her French accent.

There was constant intercourse between Young Street and North End Road. If we were not taken to The Grange my grandfather was sure to come round after tea when it was too dark to paint. When he came I always asked him to draw pictures, for which purpose a book of blank drawing paper of the very best kind was kept at Young Street. In it he drew pictures for me, each with an enchanting title. Many of the names were invented and written down before he could make the drawings, so that we shall never know now what the Fen Ganger was like, or Heath Horrors, or the Mist Walker.

My first demand, when I was nineteen months old, had been for a picture of my tiger, a preposterous stuffed beast to which I was devotedly attached. It had no merit from an artist's point of view, but my grandfather loved me so much that he did anything I asked. Accordingly he sat down with grave intent face and drew the animal with all the skill he could, putting it into a romantic landscape with a rising sun. But I was not allowed to choose a subject again, only to say which of the entrancing titles I would like him to use. The tiger was followed by a farm with a duck pond, and a great barge full of babies sailing over a neatly rippled sea. Then came a series of schools for children and animals, culminating in a Seminary for More Advanced Dragon Babies with doors leading to the Hisstry and Jogruffy schools. A page called The North Sea shows the track of some great unknown beast going down to a cold stormy sea where a darkened sun rests on the horizon under lowering clouds. The

Burning Mountain is a rugged hill crowned with a fierce upward rush of flame. Smaller fires are licking out of clefts in the hillside, a little city lies at the foot, and far away on the heaving sea a ship is being tossed to and fro. Volcanoes, especially Vesuvius, were a favourite subject, and he gave me two little early nineteenth-century volumes on Pompeii and Herculaneum, 'the cities of the burning plain'. Flames he always loved to draw. With a few lines of his pencil he gave the rapid rhythmic onrush of a fire, looking as if it had been arrested in its course and turned to beaten metal.

A lovely drawing of The Tree that Weeps has a little tree with crooked branches shedding tears from every leaf. The tears run into streams shaped like the branches of the tree, and these meet in a swift flowing river shaped like the trunk, so that the tree is imaged in its own tears. These pictures were mostly drawn after tea on winter evenings. My grandfather sat at the dining-room table with the book in front of him while the little girl made her choice among the ravishing titles that he had written on the blank pages. Best of all I remember the Mirk Strider, whom he drew at my wish one evening. I sat close up to him, watching the horror grow. With the very soft pencil that he used for this drawing he adumbrated a shadowy figure of unearthly size, clawing hands outstretched in front, hair flying backwards in the wind of its onward course, taking hills and valleys in its seven-leagued stride, a starless night overshadowing whatever evil it was bent upon.

Even if I could not remember my grandfather at all, I should have proof enough of his adoring love for me in the photographs that were taken by Mr. Stiles, our Kensington photographer, when I was two and a half years old. Mr. Stiles lived on the north side of the High Street, in a little backwater long since destroyed. To reach it you went under an archway next to Coles the carriage builder in whose shop a life-size model of a dapple grey horse dazzled the young beholder's eye. His studio, a top-floor room with a skylight, was on the left; and here we were all three brought in every stage, from fat babyhood to the awkward age. From among the many photographs of those early years I pick out three. In the first my grandfather is holding me on his knees. I am standing with a fat, rather sulky face turned away from his, which is lightly pressed against mine with a look of deep, patient adoration. In the second he is drawing something for me on a large sheet of cardboard. He is sitting on a wooden studio seat, bowed, with intent eyes, over his work. I, sitting beside him, close up against him, am following the picture with absorbed interest, my hand placed over his to guide the pencil. In the third he is still making a picture for me, but I have lost interest and am impertinently pulling his beard.

The garden of 27 Young Street was large enough for us to play in through the long summer afternoons. The Greyhound next door had unfortunately parted with its garden before I can remember, and had high ugly stables over it. As a child one naturally did not recognize the ugliness, and it was very interesting to hear the horses walking up the slope to their first-floor bedrooms, or see a long, mild, bored face looking out on a Sunday morning from a barred window. Against the stable wall a small triangular piece of ground was enclosed, with a high wall jutting out into our garden. No one knew what it was for. Occasionally a ball or a shuttlecock hit too high would bounce on the edge. If it fell inside one never saw it again. A great horse-chestnut overshadowed the tool shed at the far end of the garden. Here my father's bicycle was kept, slung by an ingenious arrangement of ropes and pulleys from the roof. The old bicycle with the high front wheel had been discarded before my time, but I can just remember my father lurching from side to side along the gravel path, acquiring the technique of the new machine.

The wall at the end of the garden was too high to climb, but the wall between us and Felday House was our constant playground. Our kind neighbour Mrs. Bowman had two little ladders made so that my brother and I could easily get over into her garden. It was my joy to get on to the wall by means of our ladder at the far end and walk all the way down, crouching under the branches of the old mulberry tree and probably getting a spattering of juice on my holland pinafore, till I reached the dizzy heights above the pantry area. The Bowmans' house had been built out at the back by Philip Webb, so that one came to their area before one got to ours. Mrs. Bowman was terrified that I might slip and break myself to pieces on the stone flags, so she spoke to my father, who made a little gallows of firewood and set it up on the wall as a sign that I was not to go any farther. So I came back again and got down off the wall and got my brother to help me in a delightful piece of work. We mixed earth from the flower bed with water and applied it liberally with a trowel to any places where the old mortar was crumbling away between the bricks. Of course it fell off at once and we got very dirty, but we felt we had done a useful deed.

Every treat we had seemed to include enormous quantities of dirt. When we went into Kensington Square we ran our hands along the railings till they were black and grimed our faces and smocks by pushing in among the sooty shrubs. An afternoon in the garden meant being washed in several waters. The occasional visit to the leads over the night nursery was an orgy of smuts. How thankful Nanny must have been when the day came for the trunks to be brought down from the boxroom at the head of the stairs and we all went off in a station omnibus to Victoria for our summer visit to our grandparents at Rottingdean.

Part Three
NORTH END HOUSE
I

MANY years before we children were born my grandparents had been looking for a house at the sea-side
where my grandfather could have the Brighton air which
to him was magically restoring. My grandmother, walking
across the downs, had come to Rottingdean and seen a white
house on the village green. This was their home for many
years, and my grandmother lived there till her death.

The original house was a three-story cottage, only one
room thick, but there was a neighbouring house standing
at right angles to it a little back from the green, and the two
houses were later made into one by an architect friend. The
whole was a most ingenious and rather confusing dwelling.
The little court or garden between the second house and
the road was built over, and formed the link between the
two houses. The result of this was that to get from one
part of the house to the other you had either to go through
a room in the connecting part or, if you did not wish to
trespass upon dining-room or studio, go right up the blue
staircase, through the nursery, and down the brown staircase. As the second house stood on a slightly higher level
than the first there was the additional complication of little
flights of three or four steps between the two houses on
every floor. It all made a kind of rabbit warren most enchanting to a child.

It was called North End House, partly after North End

Road where my grandparents lived in London, and partly because it was within measurable distance of the north end of the village street which ran up from the beach past our house and the village green, and finally turned to the right up the hill before it straightened itself out and went on up the valley to Woodendene and Lewes. The house, shiningly white all over, was divided from the road by a low white paling in front of a euonymus hedge. I can't think what the south coast would do without euonymus and tamarisk, those dismal eternal shrubs. The dull, feathery tamarisk, always coated with dust from the white roads that are cut through the chalky downs, and the sparkling euonymus, every leaf varnished to dark, or to hard yellowy green, absorbing all the softer rays of light and giving back nothing but fierce glitter. Both are impervious to salt winds and winter frosts, and when the foam is blown up from the sea by south-west gales they never shrivel a leaf or lose a young shoot.

We went in through a little white gate upon which we were forbidden to play, so we always climbed it or swung upon it when Nanny's eye was off us. On the right was a little path between hedge and house, covered deeply with the shingle that is used so much for paths in that country. Another of our forbidden pleasures was to walk up and down this path from the front gate to the fence which divided North End House from Gothic House, the boarding-house next door, kicking and shuffling the shingle with our feet. Some of it went into our sand-shoes and was very uncomfortable; the rest was left in untidy heaps till Ernest, the garden boy, came and raked it smooth again. On the

left were brick steps going down to a little area outside the
scullery window where the tradesmen delivered their goods,
and this also was forbidden to us. In fact Nanny's whole
existence seemed to be spent in forbidding things for no
particular reason. It may have been that she was not on
good terms with the kitchen inhabitants and didn't want us
to mix with them, but visits downstairs, by the outside steps
or by the more legitimate medium of the kitchen stairs, were
sternly discouraged, though this didn't in the least prevent
one's getting down to the kitchen and cleaning out the bowl
in which a chocolate pudding had been mixed, or indulging
in that peculiar passion of the young, uncooked pastry.

Between shingly path and scullery steps was a brick path
which took one in two strides to the porch. Shingle and
brick represented the two common forms of path in those
days—asphalt had not yet reduced everything to a common
ugliness—and there was a third and most uncomfortable
form of paving which was round stones about the size of a
duck's egg laid close together in tightly packed earth, or
sometimes mortared: a penitential form of pavement to all
pilgrims, but more especially to those with bare feet. When
you go barefoot all the summer your feet become hard
enough to turn the edge of a piece of broken glass, but the
hardest sole cannot happily walk on cobble-stones, neither
is shingle really comfortable. The paths that we preferred
were of brick, cool and refreshing to the feet on rainy days
and with a delicious basking warmth in sunshine, though
sometimes, on an August afternoon, too hot even for our
leathery soles, so that one was glad to walk in the gutter
where water might be running, or pad along the middle of

the road. Damp walking is very much more agreeable than dry when you are barefoot. 'Dirty and dry', was the description of the most uncomfortable feelings one's feet could have, smothered with chalky dust from the roads, or caked with the clay or mud one had acquired at the edge of a pond and then dried hard by sun and wind. The most delicious of barefoot feelings is to walk on meadow grass under flood, when the water is shallow enough to be warmed through by the sun; and another exquisite sensation is good rich mud squelching up between the toes and spreading oozily over the foot. Our cousins at The Elms who went barefoot half the year could go everywhere with impunity, but we who only took our shoes and stockings off for the six weeks of school holidays were not so hardy. Their most enviable point of superiority was that they could run over the tops of the downs without feeling the little thistles which lie spread out quite flat and close to the ground in that short herbage. While Josephine and her brother and sister could speed over flat thistle and stunted cowslip alike, we could only move with hops and shrieks of agony and were ignominiously reduced to putting on the sand-shoes which we usually carried slung round our necks for emergencies.

And now we are standing in the porch with its red tiled floor, a seat along one side and its black serpent knocker on the white door. There is no need to knock, or to pull the twisted iron bell-handle, for the door is never locked except at night, but as we have only just arrived from London there is a formality to be gone through. Already as we drove up to the house we have seen our grandmother looking for us out of the drawing-room window and now

we must ring the bell to give her time to greet us. While the
maid is answering it my grandmother will have left the
drawing-room and taken up her position at the top of two
steps, just inside the front door, and when the door is
opened we shall see her, a little, very upright figure, in
sweeping skirts, arms stretched wide and saying 'Welcome'.
Such a difficult word to say without giving it some suspicion
of affectation or a rehearsed effect, but from my grandmother the deep expression of an embracing love. She was
so small that her grandchildren began to tower over her
while they were very young indeed, but her carriage gave
one the impression of six feet of dignity and she stood as
straight as an arrow all her life. Her large eyes were clear
blue and calculated to make a child stand abashed who had
pricks of conscience about chocolates abstracted from the
drawing-room cupboard, or peaches which had been
handled till they were what William Morris used to call
'pinch-ripe'. She was a widow during the greater part of
my recollection of her, and always wore much the same
dress, very long full black gowns of velvet or satin with a
little lace. A large watch all set with chrysolites which my
grandfather had given her was always pinned at her waist.
He had bought it for its beauty in their early married days
with almost the last eight pounds in his possession. On her
head she wore swathes of soft lace, pinned here and there
with an old paste brooch, and on one hand an old diamond
mourning ring. It had belonged to an aunt of my grandfather's and had a beautiful open setting in claws of gold,
with black enamel and gold chasing on each side. 'Aunt
Catherwood' died in 1872, and the name of the friend or

relation for whom she had worn the ring was obliterated by time. Otherwise my grandmother wore hardly any jewellery.

Meanwhile our luggage was being unloaded from the omnibus that had brought us from Brighton station. It must have been a relic of early omnibus days in London, with seats beside the driver and a knifeboard on the top where one sat back to back just like Leech drawings in old copies of *Punch*. There were other buses running between Rottingdean and Brighton, but they were vastly inferior. Those from the Royal Oak were indeed drawn by four horses, but they were such thin and jaded wisps that to drive behind them was misery, and one found oneself wondering whether their bones would come right through their wretched starved-looking bodies before the journey's end, or if they wouldn't choose this journey to lie down at the bottom of the long hill and die. But though the other bus was only drawn by two horses, they were so white and so stout and competent that it was always, if possible, arranged for us to come by the train that was met by the bus from the White Horse. It came right up the steep hill into the station yard and was waiting for us at the end of our journey. We would willingly have clambered up to the seats beside the driver, but they were usually reserved for lucky grown-ups and the most we could expect was occasionally to be jammed in, between a grown-up passenger and the driver, and allowed to hold the ends of the reins when he had gathered them up. Our Nanny had strong objections to our going outside, which were partly in the general scheme of repression and partly, I must now admit, a not unnatural avoidance of the responsibility of a child with quicksilver in its legs and sea-air in its brain being loose on the roof. So as a rule we had to ride inside with Nanny and the baby, though even here were compensations, for the bus actually had a door that was shut in cold weather and straw on the floor in winter, so that it was not difficult to find romance.

The family luggage had been piled on to the roof: large black shiny dress trunks with round tops, heavy leather trunks, massive Gladstone bags, Nanny's tin box locked and corded, and, neatly sewn up in hessian and mackintosh, the baby's bath containing all her belongings. Fashions in luggage have changed as completely as everything else since those days, and I suppose Nannies and housemaids all have suit cases now and what has happened to the tin trunks I cannot say. I was walking not long ago in a quiet street in Mayfair when a very old four-wheeler came round the corner and drew up at a large house. Like John Gilpin's chaise it did not drive up to the front door, but stopped at the area gate. There got out of it a very respectable man in overcoat and bowler and to him the driver handed down a small tin trunk neatly corded which he took on his shoulders and conveyed down the area steps. I felt that I was seeing a ghost of other times, the gentleman's gentleman with his tin trunk going down the area steps and in at the servants' entrance. As the cab turned round and made for a very discreet public-house with green blinds in the windows a few doors off, the shade of Thackeray seemed to be hovering over it.

By now perhaps I had been lucky enough to be perched up in front between the driver and some friendly grown-up, with a broad leather strap across us both, much needed when the driver turned the horses' heads, and we drove down the long steep hill from the station, the bus almost pressing the horses' hindquarters. The driver held them well up, bracing his feet against the board in front, and we held on to the seat and were thankful for the strap which kept us from slithering down, especially when our legs were too short to reach the floor. Our bus had special privileges and was allowed to go along the sea front while other and inferior buses had to come and go by back streets. So we swung round to the right in Castle Square, leaving the Pavilion behind us, and there in front was the sea which we hadn't seen since Christmas, the pier, and the bathing machines hauled up from the tide. Past terraces and squares of Regency houses we clattered, delightful houses with great bulging windows overlooking the sea, some curved, some angular. Past the mysterious terrace of houses which were all black and were built, so Nanny used to tell us, of very hard coal, because the man who built them had made a fortune in it. Past Sussex Square, sloping uphill, prosperous and spacious, each house thrusting out bow windows to get a glimpse of the sea, with gardens surrounded by the eternal euonymus. There were rumours, also supplied by Nanny, of an underground passage leading from Sussex Square to the lower esplanade, Madeira Road, so called I imagine as an attraction to invalids, and we deeply envied the inhabitants.

As we drove along with the sea on our right and houses on our left, the prospect of the downs opened in front of us and far away we saw the black sails of the Rottingdean windmill which meant our journey's end. One of the many romantic parts of this journey was to see the remains of the roads that had been swallowed up by the sea, for the chalk cliffs crumble very quickly here and people still spoke of the road we were just coming to as the New Road, though it had been in use for many years. The Old Road had continued the line of the sea front, going all along the coast to Dover, but much of it had fallen away and become unsafe for wheeled traffic. In those days one could still walk upon it, a grass-grown road between grassy banks, and the horses would have been glad enough to take it and be spared the heavy pull up the hill which the new road could not avoid. Sometimes a daring passenger would get out at Kemp Town and walk along the old road, picking up the bus further on, but there was always the chance that the bus might get first to the meeting of the ways and not wait for you. In any case Nanny would never have allowed us to leave her sight, so we stuck to the bus while it swung round past the French Convalescent Home with miserable home-sick foreigners looking wanly at us from the chairs where they lay wrapped in rugs. It seemed so desolate to be French and convalescent at that windy corner and almost in sight of your native land.

Now the horses slowed down for the long pull up the first hill. My mother had what seemed to us an excessive tenderness towards horses and all country drives were a succession of dismounting from and remounting whatever vehicle we happened to be in with a view to sparing the horses, always when going up hill and often when going down, unless she had previously satisfied herself that a drag of unusual power had been put on. It was always a sore point with us that we were forced to get off and walk up the long hill and indeed I cannot think that the weight of two children of five and seven would make any appreciable difference to the horses. The only effect it had was to make us vow secretly never to get out of any carriage, however steep the hill, when we were grown-up. Another of my mother's amiable weaknesses was to make us do a kind of sitting gymnastics, supposed to be favourably received by horses. If we were going up a hill we would be adjured to sit well forward on the seat to throw the weight as near the front as possible. On the level we would have a brief respite and when we descended the further slope, the command was to lie right back so that our weight might somehow hold back the carriage. I have even known her stop a dog-cart at the bottom of a hill to shift the position of the seat, we meanwhile plodding up the hill, and then, after a brief normal ride along the level, she would have us all out again to move the seat back to a position more suitable for going downhill.

At the top of the long rise a clear expanse of country was open before us. Roedean School was still in its cradle in Sussex Square and there was nothing to break the long lovely lines of the downs. Brighton lay behind us, the gasometers were passed, and the only signs of man's handiwork that we could see ahead were the black windmill and, between us and the sea, the tall chimney that was a ventilation shaft for Brighton's main sewer, a gaunt ugly piece of utilitarianism, very different from the shaft at the other side of Rottingdean which was disguised as an enchanting little cottage, white with green shutters. Only on some days did

a wind blowing from its direction across the downs betray
what the house was meant to hide. All the rest of the way
the old road ran green and deserted between us and the
cliffs. In places it was quite broken away, but much of it was
untouched, with a little strip of grass still left between the
further bank and the sea. Only if you went near the edge
you could see ominous cracks, and the beach below was
strewn with huge fragments of chalk that had crashed down
in the winter when alternate frost and thaw were doing their
destructive work. Here and there a few houses stood
roofless and derelict, abandoned as the cliff crumbled and
fell, used as a resting-place by tramps. Presently a long
valley opened on our left and we stopped to set down a
passenger for Ovingdean which lay half a mile or so away
among trees at the end of a white road. Here my mother
would take advantage of this stop to turn us out and make
us walk up the last hill. This time we felt less resentful, for
Nanny was safely inside the bus with our baby sister and
with her eye removed we could scramble up the steep bank
of the chalk cutting, clutching at scabious and yellow
horned poppy as we climbed, and walk along the top of
the ridge looking down on to the bus. Now we came to
Greenways, the only house facing the old Dover Road that
was still inhabited. Behind it were pigsties and we could
hang over the wall watching and smelling those agreeable
animals till the bus caught us up.

Then the drag was put on, leaving those shiny smooth
marks on the surface of the road, and we skidded down hill
into the village while Charlie the conductor blew his long
coaching horn. Charlie was one of the village wits, a

tremendous favourite with all the maids. When he stood
at the back of the bus, swaying to its motion as it turned
down to the right to the White Horse, the archangel Gabriel
would have compared poorly with him in our eyes. The
White Horse was the official terminus of the omnibus,
but after delivering some parcels it would go round the
village putting passengers down at their doors. The White
Horse was a real seaside inn then, facing the sea across a
strip of grass known, from the name of its proprietor, as
'Welfare's Green'. The older inhabitants of the village
remembered when the Dover Coach Road ran between
Welfare's Green and the sea, but in our time it had all
crumbled away and only a fragment of the inner bank was
left, which would fall in the next frosts. West of the green
was a large ugly house, vaguely Gothic in style, what my
grandfather used to call 'battlemented, castellated, Blue-
beard Bosh'. Its garden wall was perilously on the edge of
the cliffs and summer after summer we would see how more
of the garden had slipped into the sea till at last the house
itself began to fall piecemeal and its remains were carted
away. In the far corner of the green was a little summer-
house of trellis, 'erected', in the words of Dickens, 'by
humane men for the accommodation of spiders', where, in the
season, a photographer took up his daily abode. His whole
stock in trade was half a dozen of those delightful triumphs
of the scene-painter's art which represent a lady and gentleman in bathing dress, or riding like Templars two at once
on a donkey, with holes to put your face through. We
would have given a week's pocket money to be immortalized
in one of these enviable positions, but Nanny would never

hear of it; and what made it the more unfair was that we had
seen photographs of Nanny and our grandmother's maids
taken in these very backgrounds. Curious dark pictures
they were, rather like daguerreotypes and taken, if I remember rightly, on tin, while for sixpence extra you could
get a richly chased gold frame.

All these delights we had to look at with envious eyes
while the bus waited outside the White Horse and then
Charlie blew his horn and we turned the corner, leaving the
sea behind us, and drove up the village street. One needed
eyes on both sides of one's head to see all the friendly shops
and houses and faces that we passed. First there was the
convent, 'Star of the Sea', peopled by nuns who had been
driven from France. They did beautiful needlework and
took boarders and my grandmother and I were once
invited to a display by their pupils, during which three
young ladies in white muslin sat side by side at one upright
piano and played an arrangement of the *Estudiantina* waltz
for six hands, a performance which did more credit to their
power of controlling their elbows than it did to the musical
qualifications of the kind-faced nuns who taught them.
Then, crossing the Newhaven Road (an easier matter when
there were hardly any motors to swoop down and kill one
at the cross roads), we came to Stenning the baker whose
buns perfumed the air, Mrs. Mockford at the little fruit and
chocolate shop which always smelt of ripe pears, Mr. and
Mrs. Champion in the Post Office where you also bought
spades and buckets, Read's Stores with the red-headed
assistant. A glimpse up the hill on to the downs and we had
reached the turning that went up past the forge to the

Vicarage and then came the butcher's house and shop standing a little back from the road where Mr. Hilder home-killed South Down mutton twice a week—meat of such juicy close-grained excellence that my brother was moved to describe the Sunday joint with tears in his eyes as 'sainted mutton'. Then the long flint wall of The Dene garden with its overshadowing elms, and on our left the field with the newly erected Drill Hall which Rudyard Kipling had imperially given to the village, beyond it the entrance to the racing stables, and finally North End House and our grandmother's face at the window.

II

WHEN I woke up in the morning at North End House the first thing I saw was an angel, pulling away the curtain of darkness to let the daylight in. It was painted on the whitewashed wall at the foot of my bed in our little attic night-nursery by my adoring grandfather. How it survived the stormy life of a night-nursery where soap and sponges are freely thrown about and to scribble in pencil on the wall is the obvious duty of any spirited child, I can't imagine, but survive it did for some twenty-five years. After my grand-mother's death the house was bought by another artist, William Nicholson, who removed the angel piecemeal from the wall and gave the fragments to Frances Horner. Her father, William Graham, had been one of my grandfather's earliest patrons, and much of Burne-Jones's best work went straight to him from the studio. Pictures, drawings, illuminated books, designs for embroidery, a piano whose case he designed and covered inside and out with lovely forms and flowers, these were among the many fruits of his mind and heart which Frances Horner possesses. She had the angel mended and framed and it now looks down on her in her home in Somerset where the artist would like it to be.

To us the two houses were known by the colour of their stair carpets as 'the blue staircase' and 'the brown staircase'. The night-nursery was at the top of the brown staircase which was carpeted with the strongest and most prickly coco-nut matting, so painful to bare feet that we always preferred to make the longer descent via the day-nursery and the blue staircase. The landing at the top of the stairs between the two nurseries was deeply romantic to us because there was a fixed ladder that led up to a trap-door. Mounting the ladder, one pushed the trap-door open with one's head and emerged into a loft full of useless lumber, cobwebs, and dust, but none the less fascinating to us, especially as Nanny had included it in her list of forbidden places. Across the landing was our day-nursery, also an attic room with a sloping wall on the outer side. On this sloping wall my grandfather had painted a picture for my pleasure, a water-mill with its large wheel, reflected in a smooth mill pond. Like all the backgrounds of his pictures it was of no real place and the evening light was the light of Avalon. There was no story about it, but a child could invent an infinite number of stories for itself and wonder what happened round the furthest corner of the picture and what monster might be lurking in the dark archway under the mill. Opposite the mill was another painting. All the walls in North End House were whitewashed and as amateur fresco painters ourselves, though in the humbler medium of the nursery chalks or a pencil, we could understand what fun it was for my grandfather to be allowed to paint on a wall unchecked. On this wall he had painted a peacock, perched on a tree, with its long tail hanging down.

Beyond the peacock was a cupboard sunk in the narrow recess between the fireplace and the wall. On the upper shelves the nursery crockery was kept and the bottom shelf was full of our larger toys, or, when emptied of toys, was a good, if uncomfortable, hiding-place for a child who didn't mind sitting like a whiting with its feet in its mouth. On the other side of the fireplace was another small recess. This was the fatal corner into which I was put when I had offended against any of Nanny's rules. It was a good corner where a rebellious child could be fenced in with a chair and left to repentance. One afternoon my grandfather came up to visit us in the nursery after tea and found me, face to the wall, expiating some sin. The sight so rent him that the very next day he took his paint box into my corner and painted a cat, a kitten playing with its mother's tail, and a flight of birds, so that I might never be unhappy or without company in my corner again. I don't know what Nanny thought of it.

In the summer we were not much in the nursery, but in winter it was a very pleasant place with a bright fire shining on the white walls. It was all the snugger for its smallness and the sloping walls which shut us in and shut the night out. It had a little bow window, rather high up, into which one could climb, and it was romantic to sit there behind the blue curtains looking out at the cold night, knowing that at any moment one could slip down on to the floor again and be in the warmth and light. Nursery bath time was delicious. The little house never had a bath-room, so we used to have our bath in front of the nursery fire, a joy that the child in the modern house has to miss. The big tin bath was brought in from the brown staircase-landing and Nanny hung towels on the fender to warm while she went downstairs to fetch a huge can of hot water from the pantry boiler. Then one of us was dispatched to the night-nursery to get the big white earthenware jug of cold water from the washing-stand and Nanny mingled the two. It was so comfortable to sit in the high-backed bath, one's feet dangling out in front, with the hot water surging up round one, and then to get out on the flannel rug in front of the blazing fire and be wrapped in a delightfully scorching towel. After being thrust into our night-gowns, red felt slippers, and red flannel dressing-gowns we were sat up at the nursery table to partake of a light refection of milk and biscuits, usually Marie or Petit Beurre. Then a scurry across the cold landing and a plunge into bed.

Down the next flight of the brown staircase and underneath our night-nursery was the bedroom which always belonged to our father and mother when they were at Rottingdean. The window looked south, straight into the branches of an ilex and was framed with jasmine from which earwigs and other people with far too many legs came on exploring expeditions into the house. It was such a little room that it held no more than two wooden bedsteads painted red, two rush-bottomed chairs, and an oak washing-stand, but it had one great advantage from our point of view. If you climbed on to the head of one of the beds you could, if you dared, drop down into a cupboard whose only opening was some three or four feet from the ground while every one else hunted you all over the house. But it wasn't often that one felt brave enough to do this, for it was just on the cards that one might be unable to climb out again and then one's shrieks would be unheard and one would probably perish miserably and be found many years later like the lady in 'The Mistletoe Bough' whose fate was familiar to us from the Christmas mummers—of whom there will be more to say later. So on the whole we preferred to go down the three steps which led to the dressing-room, known always as The Bower, a low-roofed room which had two windows, both excellent for playing in. The one facing south was wide and arched and had a high broad window-sill in which two or three children could sit. Flies and bees died very freely in this window in summer and we used to collect their corpses and throw them into the garden while we waited in the hope of seeing the race-horses next door go out in prancing procession for their daily exercise. As the ivy and the white fig-tree on the wall opposite grew and spread the horses were hidden from us, but in earlier years we could see their hooded heads, their eyes looking very alarming and showing a great deal of white through the round holes, reminding us of terrifying pictures we had seen of Brothers of Pity. The other window might really have belonged to a princess's bower in a Grimm fairy tale. It was built out over the garden and had many small panes and was brushed by the branches of a pear-tree. By opening one of the little panes one could pull a russet pear off the tree in defiance of the witch who lurked below, and birds sat on the top boughs to look impertinently in at one and ruffle their spotted breasts or preen their dark feathers with a golden beak. Any one of them might have been the enchanted guardian of magic fruit and if a blackbird had suddenly talked to one with a human voice it would hardly have been surprising.

Curtains and chintzes in The Bower were all of Morris stuffs, a bright pattern of yellow birds and red roses. The low sofa and the oak table were designed by one or other pre-Raphaelite friend of the house, or made to my grand-father's orders by the village carpenter. As I look back on the furniture of my grandparents' two houses I marvel chiefly at the entire lack of comfort which the pre-Raphaelite Brotherhood succeeded in creating for itself. It was not, I think, so much that they actively despised comfort, as that the word conveyed absolutely nothing to them whatever. I can truthfully say that neither at North End Road nor at North End House was there a single chair that invited to repose, and the only piece of comfortable furniture that my grandparents ever possessed was their drawing-room sofa in London, a perfectly ordinary large sofa with good springs, only disguised by Morris chintzes. The sofas at Rottingdean were simply long low tables with a little balustrade round two, or sometimes three sides, made of plain oak or some inferior wood painted white. There was a slight concession to human frailty in the addition of rigidly hard squabs covered with chintz or blue linen and when to these my grandmother had added a small bolster apparently made of concrete and two or three thin unyielding cushions, she almost blamed herself for wallowing in undeserved luxury.

The best sofa in the house was a massive wooden affair painted shiny black. It was too short to lie on and you could only sit on it in an upright position, as if you tried to lean you hit your head against the high back. It was upholstered in yellow-brown velvet of such rich and excellent quality that it stuck to one's clothes, making it impossible to move about, and the unyielding cushions and rigid bolsters took up more room than the unlucky users. Each bedroom was provided with an oak washing-stand of massive proportions and a towel-horse conceived on aesthetic lines but sadly wanting in stability and far too apt to fall heavily forward on to a small child, smothering it in bath towels. As for pre-Raphaelite beds, it can only have been the physical vigour and perfect health of their original designers that made them believe their work was fit to sleep in. It is true that the spring mattress was then in an embryonic stage and there were no spiral springs to prevent a bed from taking the shape of a drinking-trough after a few weeks' use, but even this does not excuse the use of wooden slats running lengthways as an aid to refreshing slumber. Luckily children never know when they are uncomfortable and the pre-Raphaelites had in many essentials the childlike mind.

Opposite our parents' room was Uncle Phil's room. It was one of the passage rooms between the two houses. You entered it from the brown staircase and found a window on your right and another door immediately opposite, a trap to the unwary as it opened directly on to three steep steps leading down to the studio in the other part of the house. The long window looking on to the grassy court-yard where the ilex grew was another of the minor

discomforts of pre-Raphaelite architecture. The not un-
pleasing original sash window had been removed and a
number of what were apparently casement windows sub-
stituted, but instead of opening outwards or inwards they
moved sideways in grooves and invariably stuck. You
know how a badly made drawer will open in jerks, first at
one side and then at the other till it sticks in a crooked
position and will neither open nor shut. So it was with these
windows, except that the crooked opening was from top
to bottom. On a sweltering August day one had to wrestle
with a window that would not open more than three inches
at the bottom, or two at the top, or at Christmas when one
wanted to keep out the south-west gale, the window would
refuse to budge and a piercing shaft of cold and wet would
devastate the room as one madly pushed -the unyielding
frame.

Uncle Phil, my grandparents' only son, my mother's
elder brother, had many gifts and great depths of affection, but he was a very unhappy man. He could have been
a distinguished painter and would have been one under a
luckier star, but two things told fatally against him. He
never needed to work, and he was cursed with a sense of
diffidence and a feeling that whatever he did would be con-
trasted unfavourably with his father's work. If he had had
to depend on himself and had worked in his own way, I do
not believe that what he feared would have happened. He
had a genuine gift for landscapes and had made a style of
portrait painting which was peculiarly his own, using
canvases about 30 inches by 20 and painting his sitter in
three-quarter length. The portrait of his father which is now

in the National Portrait Gallery is the best possible example of his gift for these little likenesses. My grandfather is standing in his white studio coat working at a large canvas with the look of patient concentration that came upon him when he was creating. The likeness is perfect and the whole atmosphere of the painter is reproduced with loving mastery. If Uncle Phil had never done more than this one portrait he could claim his place among those who have truly loved and followed art. His kindness of heart was unbounded and yet he could wound most cruelly and deliberately. There was on his mother's side, coming from her mother's family, a strain of deep melancholy and self-distrust which in some of the family was almost a disease. Uncle Phil must have suffered under this all his life and could not control it enough to keep himself from making others suffer with him. He was quick to suspect an imagined slight or insult and would say or write something which would bring the unsuspecting offender to bewildered tears. Then he would fall into depths of repentance and self-accusation that shattered every one concerned. With it all his kindness was infinite and his generosity without stint. His was one of those unhappy dispositions that can rarely be at their best with their own family, and maddening self-consciousness made him say an unkind thing through sheer nervousness, or hold back, through a misplaced pride, from saying the kind word that would have made all the difference.

When the gloomy mood was not upon him he was the most witty and amusing companion possible and reduced one to the unquenchable and painful laughter that makes the whole body ache so that one longs for death to relieve one's agony. He was a creature of impulse and if he wanted to be kind it had to be at his own time and in his own way and sometimes it was difficult to express an adequate gratitude for something one hadn't really wanted. Then his sensitive nature would feel slighted and out would come some cruel stinging word that annihilated one. But his friends—and they were very many and of all classes—cared very deeply for him and their affection outlasted all the trials that his unhappy disposition put upon it. That is why, over his ashes, the words are written *Quoniam dilexit multum.*

It may be imagined after this description that to the nursery, as to his friends, Uncle Phil was an incalculable quantity. His coming was always a fearful joy as it might mean a jaunt to Brighton with pennies to put into every machine on the pier and lunch at the Metropole, or we might find ourselves for some unknown reason in dire disgrace and be quickly shepherded from the room by a parent or grandparent anxious to avoid a scene. Not the least offence was to use Uncle Phil's bedroom as a short cut from one house to the other. Not that he minded being discovered in bed or shaving, for these were treats to which we might be invited when our luck was in, but the mere fact of our dashing through his bedroom was an implicit slight on him, showing that his existence had for the moment been forgotten by the nursery contingent.

So leaving Uncle Phil's room undisturbed we will go down the last flight of the brown staircase, the flight over which my brother once leaned too far and fell over on to his head with no evil results. At the bottom of the stairs was a choice of interests. We could stop and bang the barometer which hung by the dining-room door on the left, hoping somehow to influence the weather for the good. Or we could go straight out by what had been the front door of the brown-staircase house into the garden. Or we could visit the dining-room and possibly be invited to have a peach or fig. Or we might go down the lowest and uncarpeted flight of stairs to the cellar where the furnace for the hot-water pipes lived and Ernest dealt with the knives and boots. Or, and this was our choice at the moment, we could visit the pretty parlourmaid Annie at her work. Her pantry was to the right, below our parents' bedroom and, according to the peculiar arrangement of the house, was also the only means of getting to the smoking-room unless one went out into the garden by the brown staircase door, or the blue staircase door, or the back door of the hall passage and round by the hole where the garden roller and the hose were kept and in again by the garden door. So that if the servants were having tea in the pantry and it happened to be wet, the master of the house and his friends had to put on raincoats and go round in procession.

I have so many recollections of frenzied dashes through the rain from one door to another. If, for instance, one was in the Bower and urgently required a toy which had been left in the drawing-room, there were the following routes to be considered. You might go up the brown staircase, through the nursery, and down the blue staircase, but if Nanny happened to be bathing our baby sister at the time it was almost impossible to get past without an accusation of making a draught by leaving one door open and being called back in an awful voice which could not be disobeyed because you shut the other door so loudly, not to speak of the terrible prospect of being caught by Nanny and kept there for good on some pretext or another. It was better to avoid the nursery at bath time. Then there was the quickest route through Uncle Phil's bedroom, down the steps into the studio, out at the other door, and so down the blue staircase. But the dangers of using Uncle Phil's room as a passage have already been pointed out and if one intruded upon the studio uninvited, though my grandfather was always glad to see me, Nanny was sure to get to know of it somehow and there would be a scolding in store. A third route was to go down the brown staircase, turn to the left through the dining-room, down the steps into the hall, up the steps again into the blue-staircase house and so to the drawing-room. But if the grown-ups happened to be having a meal they had a curious prejudice against a child banging in at the door, careering through the room and hurling itself down the steps, leaving the heavy curtain that hung over the arched doorway half drawn. So that on the whole the simplest plan was to make a dash across the garden from door to door, leaving a print of wet muddy feet in the hall of the blue house and then return by the same way, leaving this time wet muddy footprints in the hall of the brown house.

Luckily for us the pantry—provided that Nanny was safely in the nursery—was always glad to see us. It possessed two objects of rare interest, namely a filter and a stuffed animal in a case. The filter was merely a conventional sign, a sacrifice as it were to some forgotten god of Victorian hygiene and was certainly never used by us. Mysterious and interesting though it was, no one who rushed in from the garden to get a drink of water was going to waste precious minutes in holding a glass under the filter's slow drip. Our more direct method was to seize a tumbler with cut glass stars on it from the shelf, hold it under the tap of the pantry sink, turn the tap violently so that water splashed up into the air and over one's frock, gulp the water and rush out again. But all the same the filter, both at Rottingdean and in London, gave, one felt, immense prestige and respectability to the house. As for the stuffed animal I can't even remember what it was—a gull I vaguely think—but in any case the most incongruous ornament possible in a house none of whose members knew anything about bird or beast life, or had ever handled rod or gun.

After exhausting the charms of the pantry we could lift the latch of the narrow door in the opposite wall and fall down two steps into the smoking-room. It was the old kitchen of the brown-staircase house and was always known as the Mermaid. My grandfather had hung over the open fire-place a painted bas-relief of a mermaid with flying hair playing with fishes in a billowy sea, so the room was called by her name. The floor was brick and so was the fire-place which was re-coloured with ruddle—the red whitewash, if one may so describe it, common in some of the southern counties—whenever it got dirty with smoke. Most of the fire-places in both houses were ruddled on occasion, and it was great fun to watch the housemaid of the moment with a little pail of the luscious compound painting it on to the bricks, an occupation in which we should have loved, but were never allowed, to participate. The fire-place in the Mermaid was not ruddled very often, for only wood was burnt there and the room was always permeated by the stinging delicious smell of wood-smoke. Wherever I smell wood-smoke I am in the Mermaid again for a moment, watching my grandfather playing draughts on the old oak table whose deep polish reflects the candles; for in those days my grandparents had only lamps and candles at Rottingdean, lamps in the drawing-room and candles everywhere else. The Mermaid was furnished like the kitchen of some delightful Dickensish inn, with a big oak settle, a solid oak table, a few massive and extremely uncomfortable oak chairs, and a large oak dresser, all of them dark with age and shining with the polish of years. The dresser was hung with gay German earthenware sent from the Fair at Mannheim by a sister of Lady Lewis, my grandparents' devoted friend. At that time it had been almost impossible to get good common pottery in England and these enchanting pots and jugs of beautiful shape and colour could be got for a few pence in any market-place in Germany. The windows and half-glazed door were curtained with bright red Turkey twill through which the fire and candlelight shone at night with the authentic Dickens touch.

Here my grandfather would come with his men friends to smoke and play draughts; games that seemed to go on for hours and hours, my grandfather sitting with intent face, pondering on a move for the length of time that a cigar would take to accumulate a long grey ash. The candlelight shone on the dresser and on the pewter jugs on the great oak cupboard behind the settle and glimmered back from the table; and a child, sitting on the bench which ran along the wall under the low windows, waited for the ash to be flicked away into the fire when a decision had been reached, or to fall unheeded if the game still needed consideration. I never saw cards played in my grandparents' house, but draughts and backgammon and dominoes were often played, mostly between tea and dinner. My grandfather rarely sought any further relaxation than a change of work. When the light was no longer good enough to work in oils he would take up a pencil, or if he had finished with his pencil he would draw in coloured chalks or water-colour. His hand and mind were never idle and these games were a rest to him in that they were a different form of absorption.

In summer the garden door of the Mermaid stood open and the draught players looked across the orchard and sweetbriar of the garden to the lovely line of the downs high above. To the left of the fire-place there was a recess with a little window of stained glass, a figure of a lute-player surrounded by bull's eyes. This was an addition not approved by the nursery, because it replaced a casement window by which one could climb in and out, a far more adventurous way than using the ever-open door. In wet weather the window was also a short cut to the cloisters. Short cut is, of course, not a good description, but to us any way that was not the ordinary and easy way of getting from one place to another was known as a short cut, so I keep the name. And coming to the cloisters, we found ourselves at the starting-point for all the adventures of the garden.

III

GOTHIC HOUSE next door was a boarding-house and North End House had all the garden of both houses. A high flint wall ran right across the back of Gothic House and its little paved brick courtyard, dividing it from our garden, and against this wall was a high penthouse roof of red tiles, known as the Cloisters, supported on plain wooden pillars set in a low brick wall. The space below the roof had a wooden floor, making a pleasantly echoing place for our wet-weather playground in summer. It contained a couple of large beehive chairs made of creaking basket-work like the 'sulkies' in the garden at Earlham. Grown-ups could sit facing each other in them and talk, or could turn them back to back and read or meditate, undisturbed by the sight of each other. Children could turn them over on to their backs and use them as cradles, or pirate ships, or Spanish galleons, or an Argo, or the Ark. Or they could pull one over on to its face and crouch beneath it in hiding from the world in general and Nanny in particular. Here also were deck chairs and a few rush-bottomed chairs, stained with paint, discarded from the studio, and in one corner a heap of outdoor toys; spades and buckets for the beach, a spotted wooden horse on wheels and the little wooden go-cart which our parents brought from Germany, christened by Jeanne, the French maid, 'le petit chariot'. It was the kind of low four-wheeled cart that dogs draw in some parts of the Continent, or children drag about in Ludwig Richter's pictures, and we used it to drag our baby sister and each other about the garden. There were moments when the

axles bent or a wheel came off and then we had the pleasure
of dragging it round by the village pond to the blacksmith
and having real repairs done while we waited. The forge
was at the far end of the pond, opposite the Plough Inn,
just where the road called Whiteway went up to East Hill.
Rottingdean was rich in public-houses; five to a village of
about a thousand inhabitants. The White Horse and Royal
Oak were houses of some size and pretension, the Plough
Inn was more frequented by farmers' men and labourers
who brought horses in to be shod, or wagons to have new
metal tyres to their wheels, and there were still the Black
Horse and the Queen Victoria—hardly more than ale
houses—to supply the needs of the public.

At the end of the cloisters nearest the house there grew a
bay-tree affording easy access to the tiled roof on which we
walked like cats with bare feet. This spot was technically
forbidden for various reasons. Nanny forbade it on general
grounds of disapproval of anything we wanted to do. My
mother had visions of our mangled forms falling six feet on
to the ground on our side, or ten feet into the boarding-
house yard on the other. My grandmother very properly
objected to a habit of using the gutter which ran along the
lower edge of the cloister roof as a final foothold, for this
gutter was of a peculiarly sacred nature, supplying as it did
the rain water for the huge butt that stood beside the bay-
tree. But in the summer holidays these restrictions were
partially removed because a barefoot child could run along
the roof to where the big fig-tree hung over at the farther
end and put the ripening figs into green muslin bags to
protect them from birds and wasps. How the faint smell

F

of the fig-tree comes back to me and the rough sticky feeling
of the leaves as I thrust among the crooked branches, exploring for half-ripe figs to be jacketed, or picking those that
were burstingly ripe and ready for the dining-room. There
were little figs that never reached normal size though they
were perfectly ripe, and they were the property of the first
child who found them. How superior are our long Sussex
figs to the short round foreign variety. My grandparents
had three trees, two purple and one white, and while their
season lasted we fed on honey-dew every day. When we
were given figs in the dining-room we had to eat them in a
special, and I think elegant, way. The fig was held by the
stalk in the left hand and cut lengthwise with a silver knife
and then lengthwise again, so that it opened like a flower
with four perfect petals spreading outwards. It was then an
easy matter to scoop out the ambrosial inside with a spoon
or the human tooth.

As one descended from the cloister roof one was apt, if in
too much of a hurry, to land with one foot in the snail-pot,
a large tin bowl with a wooden handle which lived per-
manently under the rain-water butt with a handful of salt
in it for the disposal of snails. Never have I known a garden
so infested with snails. Enormous grandfathers congregated
together in twos and threes under the roof of the cloisters
and in every angle of the wooden pergola on the other
side of the lawn. Middle-sized parents lived under every
leaf and on the stalks of every flower, while there was a
perfect congested district of tiny, brittle-shelled descendants
in every iris clump round the pear-tree outside the Bower
window. It was one of our jobs, and seldom was a useful

duty undertaken with so little reluctance, to collect these pests of society whenever we saw them and drop them into the snail-pot to die. Some children were paid a penny a hundred, but I don't think the idea of payment ever entered our heads and we hunted them down with the hunter's stern joy in the chase. What happened to the nauseous mixture I don't know. Probably Ernest, the garden boy, dealt with the corpses and buried them in the rubbish heap, but every day a fresh brew of salt and water was waiting by the rain butt for us to fill.

The whole garden cannot have been much larger than a tennis-court with plenty of room round it, but it had been so ingeniously cut up and laid out that to us it seemed infinite space. Beyond the snail-haunted pergola was a little plot of ground with trellis round it where we were each supposed to have a garden, but beyond bringing up stones from the beach to mark the confines of our separate plots, and sowing one penny packet of mustard and cress and one of nasturtiums, I cannot remember that we ever paid any attention to horticulture. We were far more interested in the brick incinerator where my grandmother superintended the garden boy burning the rubbish. She was something of a gardener herself on a small scale and had a touching faith in human nature which made her take boy after boy from the village to be 'trained'. As the training consisted of working for a couple of hours after school under her very mild supervision, with intervals for talk about books and life in general, it was hardly surprising that the garden suffered. We were used to hearing, year after year, accounts of the laziness and incompetence of this or that boy who was to have been a paragon, but it never seemed to occur to her that they imposed upon her at all, or took advantage of her readiness to read bits of Ruskin aloud to them when they ought to be working. The only time when her faith was a little shaken was the year when the very laziest and most incompetent boy of all, under whose unloving care the garden had become a wilderness, won the first prize at the local flower show for his own garden; though even then she was able to persuade herself that without her training the prize would not have been won.

My grandmother had a great deal of natural self-possession and dignity and a power of accepting every one—no matter what their social position—entirely for what they were in themselves. She could talk to working people in their cottages with as much ease as she received royal princesses who came to look at pictures. I must say that I think the first of these tasks by far the most difficult and I was always paralysed with shyness if my grandmother took me with her on one of her cottage visits. There was no condescension in her visits and no familiarity, though the child who accompanied her was ready to cry with confusion as she sat with her large blue eyes fixed on some gnarled unlettered old woman, telling her tidings of comfort from *Fors Clavigera*. Only her entire absence of self-consciousness made these visits possible and there were other and—to us— even more shameful occasions when she would have a worthy carpenter or wheelwright to the house once a week to discuss the socialism in which she so thoroughly and theoretically believed. All the snobbishness latent in children came to the fore in us as we watched the honoured but unhappy workman sitting stiffly on the edge of his chair in his horrible best clothes while my grandmother's lovely earnest voice preached William Morris to him. Then there were times when she believed that a hideous but favoured maid was worth educating. In the evening there would be an embarrassing ritual and the maid would sit in the drawing-room, though at a respectful distance, and read aloud to my grandmother from such books as she thought suitable to the domestic intellect on *The Distribution of Wealth* and the *Early Italian Painters*. How we hated it all and how uncomfortable it was for every one concerned except the kind giver of these mental feasts. There can rarely have been a woman who was so absolutely unconscious of self, though it was carried to such a pitch that even her sense of humour fell into abeyance. Now and then her humour did get the better of her, as when she described a visit she had paid to some poor family who had an invalid child 'surrounded with medals for abstaining from vices of which he was incapable'.

In spite of her wide affections and deep understanding she was curiously removed from real life and I think she honestly believed that *The Seven Lamps of Architecture* on every working-man's table would go far to ameliorate the world. She was absolutely fearless, morally and physically. During the South African War her sympathies were with the Boers, and though she was at that time a widow, living alone, she never hesitated to bear witness, without a single sympathizer. When peace was declared she hung out of her window a large blue cloth on which she had been stitching the words: 'We have killed and also taken possession.' For some time

there was considerable personal danger to her from a
populace in Mafeking mood, till her nephew, Rudyard
Kipling, coming over from The Elms, pacified the people
and sent them away. Single-minded people can be a little
alarming to live with and we children had a nervous feeling
that we never knew where our grandmother might break
out next.

To us it was far more amusing to leave our own little
gardens untended and go on through the tiny orchard which
contained at least ten apple-trees (one rumoured to be a real
Ribstone pippin), to the summer house, a two-story building
in the angle formed by two high flint walls, facing south and
east. The lower floor was concreted and used for tools, and
the top floor was reached by an outside staircase, or, more
accurately, a broad ladder. The little room above was a
triumph of pre-Raphaelite discomfort. Bitterly cold in
winter and stiflingly hot in summer, none of its windows
would open or shut properly, being, like the windows in
Uncle Phil's room, arranged to slide, or more commonly
stick, in grooves. It contained a small wooden table and
two or three wooden chairs which were suited to no known
human body. They had been designed by my grandfather
for the seats of knights at the Round Table in the tapestry
which William Morris made from his cartoons and the chairs
had actually been translated into wood by a skilful carpen-
tering friend so that my grandfather could draw them from
life. Some had round backs and some were square and there
was little to choose between them for sheer discomfort. The
seats were very high off the ground with no depth from back
to front, so that any knight who used them would have sat

like a child with his feet dangling in the air, if indeed he managed to keep himself balanced on the exiguous seat at all. The arms of the chairs were too close together to allow any one to use a knife and fork with any freedom and too high to get one's arms clear of them, and altogether a more unsuitable set of dining-room chairs for a royal dining-room can hardly be imagined. If that is how Arthur's court was furnished it is quite enough to explain the eagerness of the knights to leave their seats and follow the quest of the Holy Grail and one can only conclude that the Siege Perilous was even more uncomfortable and ill-adapted to the human frame than the seats of the other knights.

The apples in the tiny orchard were warm in the afternoon sun when we came down from the summer house. We were only allowed to eat windfalls, but much can be done to help Nature at her work, and to bump violently into a tree was not considered unfair. One had to be careful of the windfalls though, for sometimes a wasp had eaten his way in at a bruised place and as one lifted the apple from the grass there was a loud angry noise from the feaster disturbed, and a black and yellow fury came out of the apple, swift to visit his vengeance on bare arm or leg or undefended neck. The nectarines and peaches that ripened on the high wall which faced due south were also a haunt of wasps and more than once a child, cautiously lifting a peach to see if it would conveniently snap from its stalk, was overtaken by sudden and deserved retribution as the winged terror came out of its temporary dining-room. The cooking apples were grown on espaliers on one side of the path which bounded a half circle of grass enclosed by a sweetbriar hedge. The smell of sweetbriar on a hot afternoon filled the air and permeated everything. The russet apples tasted of sweetbriar and surely no apples were ever so sweet, or broke between the teeth so crisply, or held such ambrosial perfumed juice. Sweet they were to the core and there was no need to pare them, for the skin was thin and delicate. It seems to me that apples now have thick tough skins that spoil the pleasure of biting deep into the fruit. It would have been a sin to touch these apples, even with a golden knife, for every part of them was honey-sweet and perfumed with the scented briar.

Inside the sweetbriar close a tent was sometimes pitched for us in summer. I do not know why it had been bought and it was the most wretchedly uncomfortable and stuffy form of shelter that could be devised, but naturally we felt its romance deeply. It was a round tent with a rickety wooden table on two legs encircling the centre pole and it was our supreme joy to have tea in it and equally Nanny's supreme detestation. To her it must have meant stuffiness, table manners running riot, the carrying out of heavy trays, mess of milk and crumbs, overpowering breathless heat and deep discomfort, and now I think I would agree with Nanny. But to us then it was glorious adventure. One might easily be a Knight of the Round Table in his pavilion, or Saladin receiving Richard, or the Greeks before Troy, and the highly uncomfortable meal eaten reclining on a rug in the atmosphere of the Black Hole of Calcutta among swarms of flies became Alexander's feast. Or if we happened to be Cavaliers at the moment and the Roundheads were known to be approaching in force, what was easier than to slip out on one's stomach under the flaps of the tent and, re-forming rapidly in upright position, take them in the rear. We threw ourselves into the fray with all the more ardour when the Roundhead of the day happened to be our cousin, Rudyard Kipling, who lived at The Elms across the village green.

The three Kipling children, Josephine, Elsie, and John were about the same ages as our nursery three. Josephine, very fair-haired and blue-eyed, was my bosom friend, and though we both adored her father, the stronger bond of patriotism drew us yet more firmly together as Cavaliers against Cousin Ruddy's whole-hearted impersonation of an Arch-Roundhead. For the purposes of Civil War I had assumed the name of Sir Alexander of the Lake and under this title I had sent a cartel of defiance to the Roundhead, but Alexander is a long word for seven years old and the Roundhead's answer to my challenge ended with the searing words, 'And further, know that thou hast mis-spelled thine own miserable name, oh, Alíxander.' For months I went hot and pink with the memory of this rebuff. The war between Cavaliers and Roundheads raged furiously every year as long as the Kiplings were at Rottingdean, Josephine and I leading forlorn hopes against the Regicide and being perpetually discomfited by his superior guile, or by the odious way in which the Nannies would overlook the fact that we were really six feet high with flowing locks, a hat with feathers, and huge jack-boots, and order us indoors to wash our hands or have an ignominious midday rest. How would *they* have liked it if they were plotting to deliver King Charles from Carisbrooke and *their* Nannies had suddenly pounced upon them with a 'Get up off the grass now Miss Angela and come and lie down before lunch, and there's Lucy waiting for you Miss Josephine, so put those sticks down like a good girl and run along.' Fools! Couldn't they see that these were no pea-sticks, but sword, dagger, and pistol, ready to flash out or be discharged in the service of the King? But Nannies are by nature unromantic, so we had to submit and pretend to be little girls till we could meet again later.

Our Nanny had come to us when my sister was a few weeks old and though she did her duty by my younger brother and myself, she naturally put 'her' baby first and our plans and make-believes were only tolerated as they did not interfere with nursery routine. Romance in her was expressed in song. She had an enormous repertory of what had been popular songs ten years earlier and could bring tears to our eyes by 'Just a song at twilight' and curdle our blood with 'The Gipsy's Warning', or cause a wave of revivalism to sweep over the nursery by 'Beulah Land, Oh, Beulah Land'. She had a real passion for the lower forms of creation. The higher mammals she feared and loathed and never alluded to cows except as 'them vicious cows', but to any one with more than four legs her heart was open. It became an embarrassing trait, for insects recognized her as a kindred spirit from afar; daddy-long-legses in particular would come for miles to get between her stiff collar and her neck, where they spent the day in calm repose and were taken out at night with the utmost gentleness when she undressed and put out of the window on to a leaf, usually leaving a leg or two behind in the disconcerting way they

have. How very interesting were the dressings and un-
dressings of Nannies when one was small enough to share a
room with them. Their undressing of course we rarely saw
as we were asleep before they went to bed, but I have
fascinating visions of their getting up by candlelight on
winter mornings and clicking themselves into black stays
which appeared to stretch from neck to knee. It was one
of my highest ambitions to be old enough to have black
stays that clicked down the front and to imitate Nanny's
masterful handling of the mechanism; the way she fastened
them first in the middle and then with two skilful movements brought the upper parts together and then the lower
parts.

The Kiplings' nurse Lucy was also given to song and her
(and our) special favourite was a melancholy affair called
'The Blue Alsatian Mountains', which seemed to us the
most romantic thing we had ever heard. I can only remember a few hauntingly beautiful lines, or so they seemed to
me then:

> Ade, Ade, Ade,
> [this line was, of course, in German]
> Such thoughts will pass away.
> But the Blue Alsatian Mountains
> Their watch will keep alway.

It gives me lumps in my throat even now.

That summer must have been a year of song, for besides
Lucy who really looked after the younger children, there
was a governess for Josephine and that particular year
there were two. I imagine now that one must have stayed
on for a fortnight to get the other into the ways of the

house, for two governesses at once seems unusual, but the result was delightful, for they sang Mendelssohn duets together all over the downs, much to Josephine's delight and mine.

It is many years now since Josephine died one cruel winter in New York while her father too was desperately ill and her mother had to show all a woman's deepest courage in bearing what must be borne and keeping the death of the adored child from the adoring father till he was well enough to stand the blow. Much of the beloved Cousin Ruddy of our childhood died with Josephine and I feel that I have never seen him as a real person since that year. There has been the same charm, the same gift of fascinating speech, the same way of making every one with whom he talks show their most interesting side, but one was only allowed to see these things from the other side of a barrier and it was sad for the child who used to be free of the inner courts of his affection. I still have a letter from Josephine, written in sprawly childish capitals. 'I will help you', it ran, 'in the war against the Roundhead. He has a large army but we can beat him. He is a horrible man let us do all the mischief we can to him.' It must have been a very real game that made her call the father she loved a 'horrible man'. The world has known Josephine and her father as Taffimai and Tegumai in the *Just So Stories* and into one short poem he put his heart's cry for the daughter that was all to him. This letter, a nursery book which had been hers and a silver button from a coat are all I have of Josephine, but her fair-haired, blue-eyed looks and her impish charm and loving ways are not forgotten.

Although she and I were usually a devoted couple, there were plenty of quarrels. There was the terrible day when I offered to do Josephine's hair according to the White Knight's recipe for keeping hair from falling off, by training it upwards on a pea-stick, and the result was an awful tangle of yellow hair, shrieks and tears from the victim, and the descent of a governess on the culprit. Manners at meals were another subject for quarrels. Our nursery had somehow acquired the right to eat cutlet bones in its fingers unchecked, a proceeding which shocked our cousins inexpressibly and led them to call us pigs. They, on the other hand, being half American, had an odious habit of breaking their boiled breakfast eggs into a glass and stirring them up with a spoon. It was a pink glass which somehow made matters worse, and with the complete candour of the nursery we stigmatized the whole proceeding as disgusting.

During those long warm summers Cousin Ruddy used to try out the *Just So Stories* on a nursery audience. Sometimes Josephine and I would be invited into the study, a pleasant bow-windowed room, where Cousin Ruddy sat at his work-table looking exactly like the profile portrait of him that Uncle Phil painted; pipe always at hand, high forehead, baldish even then, black moustache, and the dark complexion which made gossip-mongers attribute a touch of Indian blood to him. As a matter of fact I believe the dark complexion came from a Highland strain in his mother's family, for it occurred in other cousins sharing a grandfather whose forebears came from the Isle of Skye, and two at least of them could have passed as natives anywhere in Southern Europe. Or sometimes we all adjourned on a wet day to the Drill Hall where the horse and parallel bars made splendid forts and camping grounds, and when the battle was over and the Roundhead had been unmercifully rolled upon and pommelled by small fists he would be allowed by way of ransom to tell us about the mariner of infinite resource and sagacity and the suspenders—you must not forget the suspenders, Best Beloved. The *Just So Stories* are a poor thing in print compared with the fun of hearing them told in Cousin Ruddy's deep unhesitating voice. There was a ritual about them, each phrase having its special intonation which had to be exactly the same each time and without which the stories are dried husks. There was an inimitable cadence, an emphasis of certain words, an exaggeration of certain phrases, a kind of intoning here and there which made his telling unforgettable.

Or, if it was a blazing August afternoon, we might all three lie panting on the shady side of a haystack up on the downs, a field of ripe corn rippled by the warm wind before us, with scarlet poppies and blue cornflowers gleaming among the wheat, and hear his enchaining voice going on and on till it was all mixed up in a child's mind with the droning of a threshing-machine up at Height Barn and sleep descended on us; sleep from which one was probably roused by having the soles of one's bare feet tickled with straw by way of vengeance from a slighted story-teller. Our highest heroics were apt to be pricked by Cousin Ruddy and collapse ignominiously. There was a period during which I happened to be Queen Zenobia, a role in which Josephine, who always played second fiddle in our entertainments, loyally supported me as waiting woman or

some useful super. Cousin Ruddy was cast for the part of
Aurelian, but he became mortifyingly matter-cf-fact and
wouldn't respond. The harrowing climax came when he
met the nursery procession coming up from the beach one
day, myself carrying for some unknown reason a quantity
of wet sand in the up-gathered skirts of my blue serge frock.
Queens in adversity deserve some consideration, but Cousin
Ruddy only said:

> There was a Queen Zenobia, and
> She filled her pinafore with sand;

upon which the queen dissolved in tears and became a very
furious little girl.

One winter I devoted hours of hard work to making a
book of poems for Josephine whom I dearly loved. They
were all written out by hand, but looking back I cannot say
that they had any merit at all, being poor in thought and
construction and largely borrowed from other sources. The
only poem I can remember will illustrate the graver defects
of my immortal works:

> The antlered monarch of the waste,
> Sprang from his heathery couch in haste,
> And worked his woe and my renown,
> And burnt a village and sacked a town.

Not good, you will say, and indeed you will be perfectly
right, but Cousin Ruddy, who as a poet himself should have
been kinder, so criticized my unhappy attempts that I sank
into a state of dejection which lasted several days and was
only really cured by being allowed to come into the study
and see him write his name, very, very small, with a very,
very large pen—a much coveted treat. It was his kind

custom at the end of the holidays to give me a sheet of paper covered with autographs which I was able to swap at school at the current rate of exchange for stamps and other valuables.

IV

IF I had been over from North End House to spend the afternoon with Josephine Kipling at The Elms, it was quite likely that I would find a little knot of sightseers gathered outside the high white gate which screened the house from the road. All through the summer months charabancs, drawn by four skinny miserable horses (how mysterious the word *sharrabangs* was to us), would disgorge loads of trippers at the Royal Oak, and as there was little for them to see in the village besides my grandfather's house and the church, they spent a good deal of time round Cousin Ruddy's gate. The Kiplings had been obliged to have the gate boarded over in self-defence, leaving a little hole with a sliding shutter through which you put your hand to open it. Through this hole tourists would stare with a persever-ance worthy of those individuals who looked through the grating in Mr. Nupkins' gate at Ipswich. Not once nor twice did Aunt Carrie (she had been a Balestier from Ver-mont and Cousin Ruddy wrote *The Naulahka* in collabora-tion with her brother Wolcott Balestier) have to ask a kneeling crowd of sightseers to move aside and let her go into her own house. The tourists were marvellously mis-informed as a rule and I am afraid we took a perverse pleasure in lingering near the gate and deliberately misleading any one who asked us questions, though in the case of the gentleman who wanted to know 'where Rupert Gilpin lived', but little misleading was necessary. Nor did we find it needful to undeceive the inquirer in the churchyard who asked in a hushed and reverent voice 'where Rudyard Kipling lay'.

If Nanny was not on the look-out for me with an eagle eye for escapades, there were many ways of diversifying the journey home. It is true that the journey only consisted of a few yards across the village green, but why go in that direction when there were so many friendly houses to choose from at our end of the village? Even if Nanny was on the look-out one might, instead of turning to the right and so straight home, go sharply round to the left and be lost to sight behind the Kiplings' garden wall. Then one would swing for a little on the chains which hung between posts along the edge of the road. Behind them the ground sloped upwards to a long euonymus hedge behind which Farmer Brown lived. We were personally not on visiting terms with Farmer Brown, but we stood in respectful awe of a man who had such an enchanting farmyard and such fine barns and such heaps of rich manure and could play on haystacks whenever he liked without being turned off by an irate farm hand. His older labourers remembered the time when the ploughing was still done by oxen which were turned into the yard at night.

Some of the labourers had the good looks which you find in the Saxon counties; regular features, skin of a beautiful golden brown, blue eyes, and corn-coloured hair. Curiously their wives and daughters rarely had the same good looks, but the women may have had some of the intelligence which was hard to find in most of the slow-witted slouching men.

One handsome young giant to whom we talked over a farm-yard gate was asked some question by my grandmother about his work and who was his master. 'Muster Brown I be his employer', he slowly replied and then as slowly amended it to, 'leastways he be my employer.' The difference seemed hardly worth mentioning. Others among them belonged to some older and more mysterious race, dark, thin, and hawk-faced, though with the same piercing blue eyes. The oldest shepherd was a man of this type. He would spend weeks away upon the downs with the sheep and was weather-wise beyond what is human. When one met him on the downs on a winter evening in his long cloak, his moleskin cap well tied down over his ears and his steel-tipped crook, symbol of his office, in his hand, he might have been one of the shepherds following a star. His language, to us at any rate, was simple and exalted, like one of Hardy's peasants who sound so unbelievable in print and are yet so true. One day we found him at leisure near a lambing fold, an enclosure surrounded by wattled hurdles to give the ewes some shelter from the spring winds. With a young lamb sheltered in the folds of his cloak he looked incredibly picturesque (it is just possible that he knew it), and he began to tell my mother a story about a former master, the best and kindest master a shepherd ever had, and how one day he had gone up to the house with a message and it rained and he had stood patiently wrapped in his cloak outside. Then his master had called to him to come into the porch to take shelter. 'And he called me', the old shepherd went on, 'and he said to me "Shepherd, come under the porch, out of the rain." It isn't many would have said

that to me and me in my humble garb.' Dudeney is a Sussex
name, but there must have been some alien strain in the old
shepherd, so different was he with his courtly foreign grace
from the heavier Mockfords, Snuddens, Moppetts, and
Stennings. In his later years the old shepherd developed an
embarrassing habit. Whenever we met him on the downs
he would let fall that he had just had, or was just about to
have, a birthday, or that curiously enough it was his birthday to-day. The conventions then demanded that silver
should pass between us. Also he was apt to lead up to the
subject of his crook, for which he had always recently
refused five and twenty shillings, but as we showed no
disposition to improve on this figure the conversation
languished.

Farmer Brown's house being out of bounds (I believe
that my grandmother exchanged a ceremonious call with
Mrs. Brown once a year, but we were not included), the next
thing was to cross the road and have a good stare at the skins
of vermin nailed on Squire Beard's stable door. These gave
us a hideous and fearful joy and were inseparably connected
in our minds with the meet of harriers that sometimes
dazzled our young eyes. Squire Beard was to us a distant
and rather frightening figure. Dulcia, his little daughter,
was an intimate of the nursery, but there were dozens (as it
seemed to us) of young squires, all leg and whip and spur,
who lived in an unknown exciting world of horses and
hunting. So on the whole one did not linger near Down
House, but padded on down the hill, skirting the island
enclosure of which The Elms formed a part, till one came
round again to the top of the village street—the real North

End. Here on the right was the path that led through the field called Hog Platt to the village allotments and so up to the windmill. Even in those days the windmill had ceased to turn, but the miller's house was still there, a ruinous heap, against the windmill's stone base. The windmill was so well known that it served as a landmark for ships in the Channel and for that reason was preserved long after its usefulness in its own work was a thing of the past. Gradually the house fell away, or was moved piecemeal by people who wanted stones, and its site was hardly to be recognized. The sails rotted off the mill, tramps slept in it, birds built in it, and once or twice it was set on fire, whether accidentally or not one did not know. But ships in the Channel could not do without it and it still stands, a black hulk, looking out over the newest crop of dragon's teeth, the hideous red-brick houses that devastate the hill between Rottingdean and Ovingdean.

Just below Hog Platt was hospitable Hillside, where Colonel Phillips and Mrs. Phillips were always glad to see us and always had a peach or an apricot handy. Here the atmosphere—quite different from Squire Beard's—was all of young ladies who must have been very young indeed then but seemed very old and dashing to us. The eldest sister had married Squire Beard and was the mother of our friend Dulcia and stepmother of all the long-legged horsemen, but Mary and Lilla were at home and were endlessly kind to us and took us into their long garden which ran uphill towards the windmill. They had a far better summer house than ours. It was much higher up and had a long brick staircase to its top story and when you got there it was a kind of gazebo,

perched against a high red brick wall overlooking Hog
Platt. What fun it was to sit there and watch one's village
friends going along the footpath below. There were
brothers that came and went, but they were too grown-up
and far off to enter into our scheme and it was the girls who
let us be friends with them and took us into the kitchen
garden and let us pick apricots off the long wall.

But perhaps to-day with Nanny waiting for me it was
safer not to loiter, so I left Hillside unvisited and went on
past the tiny, picturesque, and doubtless hopelessly con-
demned cottages that stood on the other side of the road.
They were flush with the brick pavement and one dropped
down a couple of steps to go into the little front room and
could almost see into the upper room as one stood in the
street. Probably they were not very fit to live in, but we
had old friends who had lived and managed to bring up
families there and it was a sad day when the cottages were
deserted. At first bills were posted on the doors and boys
threw stones at the windows, then they became ruinous and
were pulled down. Now their stones are forgotten and
their site is part of the big garden which has grown from the
old garden of The Elms and takes up the whole island.
Then as I had done my duty to myself and kept Nanny
waiting, I ran past the boarding-house and went in at our
own front door, just in time for tea in the dining-room.

The dining-room at North End House was incredibly
small for the number of people that it held, and my grandmother's greeting of 'welcome' was daily repeated in its
open-armed hospitality. It must have been the parlour of
the old brown-staircase house and where its window used to

look over the green an open arch gave on to the brick steps
leading to the hall. Over this arch hung a heavy velvet
curtain embroidered by Mrs. Morris with a figure of St.
Catherine designed by Mr. Morris.

Its long south window looked into the grass plot where
the ilex grew on a little hillock, its two stems growing apart
so that we could squeeze between them. In autumn passion
flowers blossomed round the window and just outside a bell
hung under a little wooden shelter against the weatherboard
wall of the blue-staircase house, to call us in from the garden
for meals, though really it was hardly necessary when there
was such a very deeply booming gong in the hall. The
dining-room wall was hung on the three other sides with
hangings embroidered by Mrs. Morris, from her husband's
designs; a coarse woollen material, very dark blue, with
clumps of flowers at regular intervals. The hangings on each
side of the fire-place, facing the window, masked recesses
where china and silver were kept. Here one could hide; and
whenever one was sent to get anything from the shelves
one murmured to oneself, 'She drew the arras aside'. My
grandmother had a very high-backed chair, covered with
some blue Morris material, which stood with its back to the
window and so enveloped her little form that she was almost
invisible to any one entering the room. I never heard her
discuss domestic matters or housekeeping, but Rottingdean
meals were very delicious. One remembers the lobsters that
came fresh from the Fish Woman's cart an hour after the
lobster pots had been taken up, creamy and delicate as no
town lobster is, for your lobster is something of a vintage
breed and does not travel well. The nursery was always

allowed to have the lobster's whiskers—antennae—feelers—
I don't know their right name, and they made a fine show
stuck in the ribbon of one's summer hat. Later on, when we
were allowed to join the grown-up lunch, we were promoted
to a claw and were blissfully happy with the silver lobster-
pick, rummaging down to the very tip for edible morsels.
Prawns of gigantic size we also had, in whose head Nanny
could find two little things remotely resembling figures of
people, called Adam and Eve. And shrimps of course which
we had caught ourselves, and winkles—but these were
considered low and Nanny did not encourage them.

It was a tradition which has been handed on in the family
that the wife should carve, and my little grandmother was
almost hidden by the Sunday joint. Her carving knife with
green ivory handle was worn by age almost as fine as the
rapier with which the chef in charge of the cold table cuts
the ham, and the sirloin of beef or the 'sainted mutton' fell
to pieces at once under her skilful hand. She had ways at
table inherited from her youth in the north of England,
belonging really to an earlier generation, and always ate
cheese on the point of a silver knife with extreme delicacy.
One of her favourite dishes for supper when the family were
alone was a marrow bone. It would come to table standing
up on a large piece of toast, swathed in a white table-napkin.
At the sight of it my grandmother would carefully unfold
her own napkin to its fullest extent and pin it to the neck of
her gown with a handsome paste brooch. Thus equipped,
she would dip into the marrow with a long silver implement
—it cannot have been the lobster pick, so I think it must have
been the chutnee spoon, that attenuated caricature of an

ordinary spoon—and help us all liberally to that delicious, but almost too satisfying, dish. Another habit of her youth was to lay her slice of cake between two pieces of bread-and-butter and eat them together like a sandwich which was known in North country parlance as 'matrimōny'.

Then there were special foods for cold Sunday supper which always included hard boiled eggs with their inside removed, mashed up with butter and seasoning, and replaced, and cheese straws tied up in little bundles like faggots. At Christmas there was a turkey with gilded claws sent from Cheshire by Lady Leighton Warren. This lady was a devoted friend of my grandparents' and found for my grandfather many of the country flower names which he turned to pictures in his Flower Book. Once she sent to North End House a little sea-horse, white enamelled body, gold mane, green enamelled tail, and a saddle girth of rubies, because she said it must be like the White Horse at Rottingdean, though to any one who had seen this unassuming public-house the likeness was not obvious.

In the summer holidays heaped plates of figs and peaches and nectarines were always on the sideboard, bursting and oozing with their own richness, and a child could easily appropriate one, or two, or three without the theft being noticed. A little later the sweetbriar-tasting Ribstone Pippins took their place; and later, almonds and raisins.

When we left the dining-room for the drawing-room we had to pass through the hall. It was always worth lingering here to see if any rose-water would drip from the big glass barrel which stood in a niche by the steps and then to look at the big clock which rather erratically told the days of the month and had a painted sun and moon that tottered across a starry hemisphere. Plaster casts of Della Robbia singing boys, skilfully coloured by Nora Hallé, were hanging on the wall opposite the window and there was the horrifying joy of lifting up the trap through which coal was shot down for the furnace below. It was another of the minor curiosities of the house that though there was an excellent hot-water service to heat the pipes in the studio, it had never occurred to any one to use the hot water for any other purpose, and there was only one cold water-tap (to which we shall come later) in the whole of the blue-staircase house. Near the clock the Watts portrait of my grandfather as a young man looked down on us from the wall. He was about thirty-seven then, with straight nose, blue eyes, a high forehead, and a rather long forked beard and hair of a light-brown colour touched with golden tints. The modelling of the upper part of the face which is free from beard and moustache is singularly delicate and beautiful. When we knew my grandfather his beard and hair were grizzled and he wore his beard clipped to a point, but the sensitive modelling of the face was, if anything, accentuated.

From the hall two steps led up into the blue-staircase house and the head of the kitchen stairs. In our early days Mr. and Mrs. Mounter lived in the kitchen and I cannot discover that Mr. Mounter ever did anything at all, but he had a pair of immensely long black moustaches and had been a soldier. There was a tradition in the family that Mr. Mounter had once been in the desert somewhere, marching on something, and there was no water and at last they came to a Muddy Pool and all the other soldiers lay on their stomachs and drank;

but Mr. Mounter only took a little water in his mouth and swished it round and spat it out again, and all the other soldiers died in torment and he lived to this very day. I think this story was chiefly used to discourage us from trying to drink out of the village pond, after which green and slimy draught we should undoubtedly have shared the fate of Mr. Mounter's soldier friends. My brother, being of tender years and eminently kissable was one day lured into the kitchen by Mrs. Mounter and given cakes and thoroughly hugged, after which he came upstairs yelling and when told to stop could only repeat, 'I don' *want* be kissed by person in kitchen; I don' *want* be kissed by person in kitchen.' This piece of snobbishness was only surpassed by my horrid self when, at a tea-party for village children, being told to hand round cakes, I said in a fat sulky voice, 'I'm not a servant', which so horrified my grandmother that she was unequal to any kind of blame.

It was on the whole safer then to avoid the kitchen and pass along the passage to the drawing-room. When I think of the drawing-room at North End House I think of a very little girl wrestling with a stiff door handle till the lock rattles, one of those brass handles that are meanly and miserably small so that they give you nothing to hold and you can turn them in any direction without having any effect and it is enough to make you give up in despair if you are small enough, but some one will nearly always come from inside and open the door for you. Sometimes it is summer and the windows are wide open on to the village green and the grey church opposite is bathed in afternoon light. Sometimes it is winter, the heavy curtains between

the two halves of the drawing-room are closely drawn, and
in the inner room a fire is gleaming on the ruddled hearth.
There is holly behind the pictures and there are rumours
of a play about St. George to be acted after tea. But if we
are to look at the room, this quiet sunny afternoon at the
end of summer will be our best time. My father and grandfather will be smoking in the Mermaid and my mother and
grandmother are reading, and if I disturb no one I shall be
allowed to wander about and look at things.

Just behind the drawing-room door is the little upright
piano which after many years found its way to South
Kensington Museum to spend the rest of its life there. Even
in those days its musical life was near its end and it would
only make a sad cracked tinkling, but it had been designed
by my grandfather to show how a cottage piano needn't
necessarily be a lump of hideousness. It was a simple, un-
pretentious shape, made of plain wood stained brown, and
on it my grandfather had painted a picture of girls playing
in a garden and Death, veiled and crowned, scythe in hand,
knocking at the garden door. The piano he had designed
and painted for Frances Horner was richer and more
beautiful, but this early work had a more touching if less
assured beauty of its own. The design of musical instruments was of great interest to him and he had carried out
several other large pianos constructed on the lines of the
harpsichord, that is to say, a case in harmonious relation
with the lines of the strings, tapering away towards the end,
instead of the rounded monstrosity of the ordinary drawing-
room grand, and legs that were elegant and serviceable
instead of merely elephantine. Broadwood made these

pianos for him and my parents had one of them for many years, with an oak case stained green and green ivory keys instead of black. It is now in the Royal College of Music, its own music nearly dead, but a mute testimony to the fact that a piano needn't be a blight upon a beautiful room. This piano and a harpsichord by Broadwood and Tschudi stood for years in the same room and they had the same distinction of line and the beauty that comes from complete harmony between soul and body—the chords that make the music and the case that holds them. Another of his experiments was the case of a clavichord which Arnold Dolmetsch made to his design. He painted the outside a deep red like Chinese lacquer and on it in white letters a poem in Latin which my father wrote, and in a laurel wreath the words CLAVIS CORDIUM, a pun on Clavichord. It was made for my mother, so there was a picture of St. Margaret leading her dragon. Inside, under the strings, he painted a girl gathering flowers.

As for the little brown piano in the back drawing-room at North End House, we never dared touch it without permission. Sometimes, before its voice was too old, my grandmother would sing to it. Italian songs from the collection called *Gemme d'Antichità*, or English songs from Chappell's *Popular Music of the Olden Time*, or songs whose provenance we never knew, among them a song whose only words, repeated again and again were:

> Why did my master sell me,
> All on my wedding day?

My grandmother was devoted to music, though without special training, and used to amuse herself by finding pieces

—often most unexpected—of classical music to fit poetry that she loved. She had a manuscript book of these songs, a few of which I remember. One was Rossetti's 'Song of the Bower' sung to a Schubert waltz (the one that became so hauntingly familiar in *Lilac Time*), and another, Keats's 'Drear Nighted December' surprisingly and effectively mingled with the trio from the slow movement of Beethoven's Sixth Sonata. Schubert's songs she knew nearly by heart and both she and my grandfather were devoted to Gluck, largely I think through Giulia Ravogli whose Orfeo had ravished them both.

Round the drawing-room, but rather high for a child's vision, hung paintings for the Sangraal tapestry which Morris carried out. They were only a few among the hundreds of designs that he made. There are notebooks filled with sketches of a hand or a head or a piece of armour in many different positions, and even so there were also pictures upon pictures until the real picture, seen in an hour of insight, was forced to take its own shape on canvas. The Call to the Quest was there, the Arming of the Knights, the failure of the knights whom sloth or love kept from sight of the Grail, and the vision of the Sangraal which only Galahad might see while Bors and Percival kneel patiently at a distance. The story of the Sangraal was with him all his life and countless were the drawings and paintings he made for it. His only incursion into the theatrical world was the designing of scenery, dresses, and armour for Irving's *King Arthur*. Some of the beautiful pieces of armour which were made from his drawings were kept as studio properties.

Three Houses

In the larger part of the drawing-room was my grand-mother's toy cupboard. Originally begun as a toy cupboard for our visits, it had gradually fallen into her far worthier hands and she kept it and added to it with the collector's passion. When the oak cupboard was unlocked what an enchanting sight was there. It was like a page from Nutcracker and Mouse King, or a story from Ole Luk Oie. Tiny houses, gardens, hedges, and people. Russian families of painted wood, shutting up one inside the other from grandfather to baby. Merry-go-rounds that made a little tinkling noise as one turned the handle. Tiny shops and stalls with suitable apples, pears, carrots, turnips, and cauliflowers. Flocks and herds that knew no other grazing lands than the table-cloth. Fishes of mother-of-pearl from Chinese seas. Sicilian carts drawn by bedizened oxen. Saucepans and jugs and coffee-pots carved from wood, no bigger than a baby's finger nail—and whatever more of littleness you can imagine. Her friends used to add to the collection and any one who came to Rottingdean bringing some tiny tree, or flower, or figure, was doubly welcome.

On each side of the fire-place was a frantically uncomfortable pre-Raphaelite sofa, too short for any one but my little grandmother and inconceivably hard. Above them hung pictures of the archangels, Gabriel with the lily, Raphael who cares for children, Uriel, Azrael, Chemuel. But when it came to Lucifer there was only a black opening in the walls of heaven near where Michael stood, with tongues of flame licking up from the pit. It made one stand rather quiet for a moment and then one turned and climbed up on to the window seat.

V

THE window seat in the drawing-room was a perfect place. With the hard oblong cushions one could build a fort, or make an omnibus, and my brother and I could sit perched up one at each end reading, just far enough apart not to be able to kick each other. But chiefly, built out a little from the house as it was, it afforded unrivalled opportunities for observing village life. Through the side window my grandmother had kept her watch for us as we drove up to the house and from the large middle window she smiled her welcome. Let us look through the side window, the one that faces south. There is not much to see just now as we look down the village street unless it is the form of Mr. Thomas of the Royal Oak waddling up on some errand. Mr. Thomas's legs were so short in relation to his stout body that he was called Trunky Thomas by the primitive population and by us when Nanny wasn't listening. Or old Mr. Ridsdale might be strolling down the road, looking like a patriarch with his white beard, velvet coat, and peculiar soft hat, shoulders a little bowed and hands clasped behind him, accompanied by his little grandson Oliver Baldwin who rejoiced the village by falling unconsciously into an exact reproduction of his grandfather's gait as golden hair walked by white hair.

The sight of Mr. Ridsdale and Oliver made us move to the middle window to study the further movements of the Ridsdale family. Their house, The Dene, also faced the green, at right angles to ours, and in the summer it overflowed with children and Nannies. Our mother's cousin

Three Houses

Stanley Baldwin had married the elder Miss Ridsdale and every year they came down from their home in Worcestershire to spend some weeks at Rottingdean. What with babies and Nannies and luggage, they were such a large party that Cousin Stan used to have a slip coach for them which was shunted somehow from Stourport to Brighton. This impressed our young imaginations tremendously, as did the fact that an extra wing had to be built on to The Dene to accommodate them. When Cousin Stan was married I was to have been a bridesmaid in a muslin bonnet with one pink string and one blue, but on hearing the organ I shrieked so loudly that I had to be removed. Their wedding day, the twelfth of September, was always celebrated at Rottingdean and we used to write a wedding ode to them yearly. I can only remember one, which ran as follows:

Beautiful Cissie and Stanley bold,
Seven long years have not made you seem old.
Your hands are beneficent, bounteous and kind,
And the hearts of your fellows with sweetness you bind.

My father and mother's wedding day was a few days earlier and just about this time there was always a great picnic on the downs. Mrs. Ridsdale hired a farm wagon for the afternoon and a carter to lead the lumbering horses, and into it dozens of children and nurses were packed with the baskets of food and two great elephants of cart horses with feathery legs dragged it slowly up to Height Barn while the older children walked, or distracted their parents by climbing on the wagon or hanging on underneath. It was always a golden harvest afternoon when we went slowly up the road among the chalk ruts, along by the low flint wall covered with many coloured lichen. On the left the stubble lay white in the sun with a few poppies still blazing among the corn stooks. Then we were on the open downs, on that short springy herbage that makes walking a delight and nourishes the sainted mutton so well, and began to look abroad over the world. East Hill away across the valley on our right, Saltdean, where there used to be steps cut in the chalk cliff down to the beach, hidden at the end of a valley, Brighton racecourse standing out far behind us, the wind-mill brooding over the village and the road beneath winding away to the clump of dark trees that marked Woodendean, while ahead of us, a vision of enduring peace, was the perfect outline of Height Barn. Nothing but a large flint barn with tiled roof, but, through its absolute fitness in place and design for its destined work, drawing every line of the downs to converge together upon its perfect self.

Behind the barn was a deep hollow known to us as Wedding Hollow. It was too deep for a dew pond and I have no guess as to its origin. At its brink the horses were stayed and we all trooped down the winding path that led among gorse and blackberry bushes to the bottom. The nurses spread the rugs and unpacked the food and we settled down to our business of eating and playing till it was time to pack into the wagon and ride slowly home again, dropping the party one by one at their respective homes, till last of all the Baldwin children were decanted at The Dene.

The personality of Mrs. Ridsdale was the life of The Dene. Who in Rottingdean does not remember her sailing down the village street, commanding of figure, a large

silver-topped leather bag always hanging at her side, a word
for every one, an eye to every one's business, and always the
first to do a kindness? A person too of immense character.
Was it not she who invented and carried out the questionnaire
for Kipling-hunters? 'Can you tell me where Rudyard
Kipling lives?' a tourist would ask. Mrs. Ridsdale would
stop and fix him, or her, with her shrewd eye, saying, 'Have
you read anything of his?' Very often the answer was No,
when Mrs. Ridsdale would remark, 'Then I won't tell you',
and pass majestically on. The first characteristic of the Ridsdale family which struck an outsider was their alarming
frankness of speech with each other. As children we used
honestly to be a little afraid of being sent on a message to
The Dene in the morning. The family of father, mother,
three grown-up young gentlemen and one grown-up young
lady (for Cissie Ridsdale was married to Cousin Stan and
away in Worcestershire by then) would be sitting at breakfast still. In any other family the torrent of criticism and
plain speaking which burst out would have meant a violent
family row. But with the Ridsdales it was merely a family
conversation and though we knew it to be so, we were not
the less alarmed and lived in some kind of expectation of
immediate bloodshed, so that it was a relief when a diversion
occurred. Perhaps old Mr. Ridsdale would take us to his
study, a low dark room full of Indian curiosities and prickly
fish and books. He was a mysterious and rather alarming
figure to us, but always very kind, and whenever we met him
in town he took us straight to a toyshop and bought us a
toy, and what more can a grown-up do?

Or kind Lily Ridsdale would carry us off to the garden to

play croquet, or to her sitting-room where, on winter evenings, she would play the piano indefinitely for us and the Baldwin children while we sang such time-worn songs as 'Where did you get that hat?', or 'I'm a Prima Ballerina Assoluta', or 'The Man that broke the Bank at Monte Carlo'. Or there was the excitement of a visit to the billiard-room upstairs with those charming coloured balls to play with and the chance of being horribly teased by one of the grown-up brothers who were not too grown-up to enjoy lashing a little girl into a frenzy for their amusement.

The Ridsdales had been in Rottingdean long before my grandparents came. They remembered the village in the early days when there was no water except that supplied by a donkey who walked round about with pails filled at the village pump which stood in the angle of Trunky Thomas's barn and cowsheds on the village green. Those were the days when the Dover Coach Road still ran to the south of Welfare's Green and the miller was living in his little house below the great sails of the windmill and the winter storms brought strange cargoes to Rottingdean beach. One wintry week of south-west gales cast up a bullock and a baby, rapidly followed by a whale and a grand piano; but the glory of Rottingdean was the day that a cargo of brandy came ashore and messengers were sent all over the country on horse and on foot with the happy words, 'Free drinks at Rottingdean'. On another occasion the beach was again covered with casks and the messengers were sent out, but it was all an idle dream, for the cargo was paraffin oil. Rottingdean was certainly concerned in the smuggling trade in still earlier days and there were caves in the chalk cliffs which no one entered. One indeed was shut with an iron door, an object of immense interest and terror to us. There were rumours too of an underground passage leading from the old Vicarage to the beach with an outlet in one of these caves, but of this we never had proof.

The Dene possessed the first telephone that reached Rottingdean and the first we had ever seen. It was the kind that you had to wind up with a handle for a long time before it would start and you had to hold the combined receiver and mouthpiece in a tight nervous grip to keep it connected, so that you were nearly paralysed if your talk lasted any length of time. It was one of our treats to be allowed to hear Mrs. Ridsdale telephoning to Brighton.

Rottingdean must have been well abreast of the times, for not only did it introduce us to telephones, but to our first motor. From our eyrie in the drawing-room window we could see on the other side of the green the Kiplings' motor pawing the ground before the door. It was one of those incredible machines raised high from the ground with a door in the middle of the back and it didn't like starting and when it had started it didn't want to stop, except half-way up a hill, and it perpetually ran dry on the tops of lovely downs miles away from even a dew-pond and when the grown-ups went in it the ladies wore tweed motor caps of gigantic size with veils swathed tightly round them and stuck through with enormous hatpins. When we saw the Kipling children dancing round it, we were consumed with longing to go and dance too, so slipping from the room we ran across the green and kicked up the dust with bare feet to express our joy. Finally the majestic machine got under

weigh and drove off with a trail of smoke and smell behind
it and we were left lamenting. To the best of my remembrance I never went for a drive in the monster, because
whenever a ride had been promised it refused to go and we
sat and sat in it while the chauffeur tinkered at its inside and
then had to get out with a promise for a real ride some day.
But 'some day', as my brother very truly remarked, 'is in
the days that never come.' Just at this moment the young
Kiplings were descended upon and carried off by a horde of
nurses and governesses and we betook ourselves to the
churchyard for further entertainment.

The grey Saxon church faced our grandparents' house
across the green and stood on a slight slope. As in most
country churchyards the same names occurred repeatedly
on the graves; Mockfords, Moppetts, Dudeneys, Carpenters,
Snuddens. It was not always safe to wander in the churchyard, as Bowles the sexton was apt to chase one away and
had a religious belief that bare feet were unsuitable to con-
secrated ground (a belief shared by Nanny). But as he was
luckily working on the north side of the church, up against
Farmer Brown's muck-yard, we were able to slip round to
the south side and contemplate that sinister family tomb
which gave the names and qualifications of all the family
except one sister, after whose name was nothing but the
word OBLIVION. There was another terrifying tomb which
said, 'I AM HIDING IN THEE', and we always had visions of
what might come out of it towards dusk. The corner to the
south of the porch was as yet untenanted and there my
grandfather was to lie and a little great-granddaughter near
him, and at last my grandmother's ashes.

Three Houses

Now, a little sobered by our sojourn among the tombs, we waited till Bowles's back was turned—for he was a strict Pauline and I had no hat—and went softly into the church, all hung with fruit and flowers for Harvest Sunday, with a great sheaf of corn below the pulpit. We always had a feeling that the little church was part of family life, because the East end was made glorious by seven of my grandfather's stained-glass windows. As we mounted the chancel steps the Tree of Jesse was on our right, beginning with Jesse asleep at the roots and spreading its branches through David with his harp, Solomon holding a little temple, Hezekiah with his sundial and so up to the humble Mother and her Baby enthroned on the topmost boughs. Opposite was Jacob's ladder, where angels went up and down between earth and heaven. My grandfather and William Morris worked on all the windows together and as long as they both lived the standard of noble form and rich colour was unsurpassed. As with so much of Morris' work, the master's hand was needed and after his death, followed so closely by my grandfather's, windows were still carried out from Burne-Jones designs, but they were never the same. Their most glorious joint work was the great windows of St. Philip's Cathedral in Birmingham where reds and blues are a deep flaming beauty and every line in the leading of the glass is a master's line. The windows at Rottingdean are not so stupendous as these, but they are perfect in their way.

A little further on, just before the altar, was another pair of windows facing each other, St. Mary and St. Margaret who was there with a thought of the artist's own daughter Margaret. They are in deep blue, St. Mary standing quietly

alone, St. Margaret leading her conquered dragon on a cord.
Above the altar were the three windows which my grandfather gave for his daughter 'in hac aede feliciter nupta'; a
triptych of angels. To the left is Gabriel with the lily, to the
right Raphael with his pilgrim staff, and in the middle
Michael the archangel pinning the dragon with his lance, his
helmet cast aside. Below each angel is a little picture of his
doings; Gabriel bringing his lily to the Virgin Mary,
Michael fighting the grisly coils of the worm, and Raphael
leading a little child who walks confidingly by his side with
quick steps, holding his hand, with face upturned to his
heavenly companion. My grandfather returned to this picture when he had a silver seal made for me with a green ivory
handle and on the seal the engraving of an angel leading a
child by the hand across a hill under a starry sky. One of the
great differences between my grandfather's stained-glass
windows and others was not only the colour—for Mr.
Morris was largely responsible for that—but the skilful use
of the lead between the pieces of glass to build up the design.
The leading seemed to follow the flowing line of his pencil
and never cut across or disturbed the unity of the picture.
That is, I think, where so many glass designers fail.

Here we could stay in peace, feeling more than we could
understand, till our inconstant minds were as full of beauty
as they could hold and the prickings of conscience for our
unauthorized outing began to make themselves felt. Then
we went down the nave into the sunlight and saw the white
porch of our home waiting for us across the green and so
back to the drawing-room.

Four months later the drawing-room would see very

different sights. It would be Boxing Night and we were all seated in the inner room waiting for the mummers. Rumours of splendid preparations for their entertainment were afoot— supper for them in the dining-room with a gigantic pork pie and quantities of cider. A knock was heard at the door heralding their arrival and the audience began to wriggle on its seat with anticipation. Then noises and bumps and murmurs were heard from behind the curtain and clumpings on the bare boards (the Morris carpet had been rolled up and put away for the evening), and at last, just before we burst with curiosity, the curtains were drawn and the play of St. George and the Dragon was shown to our enchanted eyes. The actors could make but little attempt at dressing-up. They were poor labourers and most of them wore smocks and leggings with a few ribbons and pieces of coloured paper to adorn them. The smock-frock was still worn in Sussex by the older men when I was a child, and some of them had venerable furry top-hats. The play proceeded on its usual course, St. George, Turkish Knight, very unfeminine princess, Dragon, and Doctor; it has often been described. At the end of the play they took their customary toll of the audience:

Here come I little Devil Doubt,
If you don't give me money I'll kick you all out.
Money I want, money I crave,
If you don't give me money I'll kick you all into your grave.

But after this they added an epilogue of their own contriving. They stood in a circle all facing inwards—a method much to be recommended for shy performers—and sang, not as you might archaeologically hope, old Sussex carols and folk-songs, but ballads about Lord Raglan and the Crimean War. Folk-songs in the making perhaps. And then, because of Christmas time, the 'Mistletoe Bough', with a rough attempt at harmony in the last melancholy lines of the chorus,

> O-oh, the mistletoe bough,
> Oh, the *mistle*-toe bough.

The long-drawn tale of the Baron's young bride who invited the guests to play hide-and-seek on her wedding night and then got into a chest and was never discovered till years later when:

> The skeleton they found mouldering there
> Of the bride who had formerly been so fair,

chilled our young blood and was directly responsible for nine-tenths of our nursery nightmares.

But at last even this horrible joy was over and the mummers went clumping away to the pork pie. I remember, for memory has her tactless moments, that the back drawing-room windows had to be opened wide to let out the smell of unwashed corduroys, and the cold night wind rushing in made the candles gutter in their tall brass candlesticks. Then a sleepy child was sent up to bed and fell asleep to the sound of the revellers' voices below.

Christmas at Rottingdean began by the arrival of the turkey with gilded claws, which came by the omnibus, together with a great sheaf of holly and mistletoe. We were allowed to help with decorations, sticking bits of holly in behind pictures (the scratching noise of holly leaves on whitewash sets my nails on edge even now), and tying mistletoe over the kitchen stairs and in the nursery. For a week beforehand the waits had been about the village, frankly blackmailing the inhabitants by the horrid noise they made. There was no romantic Christmas atmosphere about them. I don't suppose any of them knew any carol beyond a very garbled version of Good King Wence as in which they always telescoped the last two bars into one, making two crotchets and a minim out of two minims and a semibreve on the word 'weather'. There were no relics of folksong here, no hymn to Woden dressed in Christmas guise and handed down from father to son, no Christmas ballads whose words were 'outway rude' though their tunes were modal, and no reverence for Christmas except as an easy way of getting sixpences. Six or seven village boys would join together with a lantern and come up the street murderously rattling through Good King Wenceslas. Nearer and nearei they came till at last we could hear the click of the front gate and the shuffli g of feet in the porch. Then the real spirit of tradition got loose in the following hymn or canticle sung at a rattling pace with an accelerando to the fortissimo on the knocker.

> May God bless
> All friends here,
> *f.* With a Merry, Merry Christmas
> And a Happy New Year.
> *cres.* Pocket full of money,
> Cellar full of beer,
> *ff.* Merry, Merry Christmas
> And a Happy New Year.
> BANG, BANG, BANG on the knocker.

When the parlourmaid went to the door a shrill chorus of

voices demanded 'Shilling for the waits, please Miss' and the message was brought to the drawing-room, which was only too thankful to buy immunity at the price of a couple of shillings. Hardly waiting to say thank you, the vocalists dashed off to blackmail The Elms or Hillside.

One year Lily Ridsdale, the younger daughter at The Dene, trained a sewing class of village girls to sing carols in parts and then it was very different. A little girl tucked up in bed heard mysterious voices out of the dark singing, 'From far away we come to you', the carol for which Mr. Morris wrote the words with the double refrain:

The snow in the street and the wind on the door.
Minstrels and maids stand forth on the floor.

The far-off beauty of the mingled parts from the cold night outside was a thing she never forgot. As she lay listening in a little room with the fire flickering on the whitewashed ceiling and a long limp stocking pinned to the foot of her bed, knowing that to-morrow morning it would be full and lumpy, it was almost too much happiness to bear.

It was a point of honour to wake very early on Christmas morning and on that one day Nanny relaxed her stringent (and well-advised) rules about lighting candles ourselves and I was allowed to grabble for the matches when I woke and light my own candle and look at my stocking. There was something unspeakably satisfying about the feel of a well filled stocking stuffed with lumps of all sizes and shapes. Cubic lumps, spherical lumps, lumps in crackly tissue paper, lumps that might be penknives and sometimes a dormouse curled up all stiff and cold. Dormice were a recurring Christmas gift because last year's usually got lost.

One dormouse, woken by the unaccustomed warmth of Christmas Day, came alive, leaped from my hand and disappeared. I was disconsolate and another dormouse was got to replace it and weeks afterwards the original dormouse was found curled up asleep, quite well, under a heavy pile of blankets in the linen-cupboard. Another dormouse escaped—my own fault alas! I forgot to put his water-tin back and he squeezed out through the hole—and drowned himself in the nursery slop-pail. I cried bitterly till my grandparents let me bury him in the garden among the lilies of the valley and my father drew me a picture of his little form with wings flying to Paradise, with earth spread out far below, and I coloured it with the nursery chalks and my grandfather had it framed in a carved and gilded frame— or at least it looked like that. But live stock was on the whole a rarity and the lumps were mostly inanimate, and always in the toe of every stocking was a tangerine orange. Nothing else would do.

.The ritual of the morning was that my brother and I should bring our stockings into our grandmother's bedroom and examine them there. Her bedroom was over the drawing-room and had a big window facing east like the window in the room below. Through it she could see the sun rise over the brow of East Hill until elms growing taller on the other side of the green made a jagged edge where once the line of the downs had stood out clear cut against the dawn. But we were with her long before the winter sunrise, climbing on to her bed, an oak four-post bed with curtains of the most delicate Madras muslin, soft enough to go through a wedding ring and so exquisitely patterned that one of her grandchildren wore dresses made from them twenty years later. In my remembrance she always used very fine cashmere sheets against the cold, and even in bed had lace on her head and the softest shawls pinned with a paste brooch. It was so cold getting out of one's own bed by candlelight in front of a black fire-place, that one could hardly wait to put on dressing-gown and slippers, and then we dashed into our grandmother's room where the fire had been kept in all night and my brother got in beside her with his sock, while I made a nest for myself at the foot of the bed with my stocking. I usually brought with me a couple of gingernuts which I had taken to bed the night before to make them soft and malleable. On any other morning it would have been my pleasure to roll them into sausages, or mould them into balls, or into a likeness of the human face, but this morning even they might be left unheeded, for there were better things to do.

How delicious it was to plunge one's hand deeper and deeper into the stocking, pull out the presents, tear off the tissue paper and gloat on the reindeer gloves with fur lining, the necklace, the little fan, the tiny Prayer Book with print that no human eye could read and Sir Joshua Reynolds' angels stamped in silver on the cover (how perfectly beautiful one thought it then), the pastels, the box of round chocolates sprinkled with sugar, and always at the end the tangerine, so cool to the touch, so sweet to the mouth, and even after you had eaten it, still useful for fireworks. You pinched a piece of the peel sharply, very near the candle and little spurts of oil from it caught fire for a moment and flashed through the flame.

Three Houses

After so much emotion there were sausages for breakfast as if it were Sunday, as indeed it sometimes was, and—we must have been an extremely lucky nursery—heaps of presents on the dining-room table. All the things that were too big to get into our stockings, things like books and engines and bricks and a real carriage-clock of one's own and always something very magnificent from Uncle Phil like a Punch and Judy Show that we could work ourselves, or a fort with a drawbridge, fully garrisoned, or one's favourite poet (Longfellow that year, Browning next), bound in blue or green morocco with one's name in gold on the cover, or quires of notepaper from Asprey's with monograms in gold and silver and all colours.

This second wave of emotion carried us on to church time. As far as I can remember we never went to church in London, except the Abbey, which is different, but always in the country because of not hurting the Vicar's feelings, so on Christmas day the family, represented by the women and children, turned up in full force. I had on a green woollen frock from Liberty's with an embroidered yoke, a brilliant red woollen jacket, a blue tam-o'-shanter, and my new reindeer gloves which it took me the whole length of the service to get properly buttoned. How we enjoyed singing in the church and how delightfully Lily Ridsdale's voice sounded and how infinitely more we admired the peacock yell of Miss White, the village laundress, and how nobly Mr. Sanders the carpenter demeaned himself on the organ. Then there was the fun of saying 'Happy Christmas' to every one, lunch, the turkey with its gilded claws and general repletion.

After a decent interval the Curse of Christmas descended upon us in the shape of thank letters. My brother and I had written a quantity of blank forms in trusting anticipation of a good haul of presents, more or less in this form:

Dear . . . ,
    Thank you very much for the . . . It is a lovely . . . and thank you so much for it. I hope you had a very happy Christmas.   Your loving . . .

But unluckily a rather hurried caligraphy made 'much' look like 'muck' and most of the thank forms were confiscated and destroyed. What a brooding nightmare thank letters are to children. One can't tell them not to write, but when I get letters from my nieces running more or less as follows:

Dear Aunt Anglia (or Angelia),
    Thank you so much for the lovely necklace. It was a lovely necklace and I do like it so much. We had a lot of presents. Now I must stop with love from Mary,

my heart aches for the tedious time they have spent on this and other thank letters.

After dark my brother and I were sometimes allowed, for a great treat, to go into the studio, which was as a rule forbidden ground. To reach it you went up the blue staircase and turned off past the linen-cupboard through a bamboo curtain. It was impossible to get a north light at North End House, so the studio faced east as the next best thing, but the light was never suitable for oil painting and my grandfather mostly worked in charcoal, pencil, or watercolour when he was there. There was an extravagance in his nature which loved to make pictures in a medium that would not last; to make a lovely or impish drawing on the back of a sheet of notepaper which some one else would use for a business letter, to paint birds and beasts and angels on a rough whitewashed wall where they would be rubbed and scratched. Among the exquisite letters with coloured pictures which he wrote to me as a very little girl, many are written on scribbling paper which was not good enough to wrap up groceries and have only been kept from falling to pieces by extreme loving care. Every year he made a sacrifice to art on my father and mother's wedding cake. A large cake, smoothly iced with pure white icing was brought into the studio on a board and laid on the large table. On it he painted a picture of the church, or the downs, or fat babies with a cat, or a pond with ducks, all in water-colour so that we could eat it without any damage.

When we left the studio to go upstairs to bed we went up by the blue staircase, past my grandfather's bedroom hung with Arundel prints and Baring-Gould's *Lives of the Saints* over the mantelpiece, and past my grandmother's room, lingering a moment on the landing before attacking the last flight to our warm nursery. On this landing all the un-self-consciousness, all the discomfort, and all the beauty of pre-Raphaelitism was epitomized in a small space. Just at the foot of the top flight of blue stairs a zinc-lined cave had been built out from the wall with a tap in it for the use of the housemaid. There was no attempt at concealment inside or out. From the outside this preposterous square excrescence was stuck on to the back of the house, looking ready to fall off at any moment, and from the inside there it was, obviously a housemaid's sink, with no disguise, and the water coming in from the Brighton main made a roaring that filled the blue staircase. Above the bold-faced sink was a stained-glass window of jewelled brilliance, containing four scenes from the story of the Sangraal; the summoning of the knights, the adventure of the Sangraal, and at the end the holy cup itself, guarded by angels in Sarras. The Holy Grail above a housemaid's sink, both needed, both a part of daily life. It is easy to laugh a little, but there was a splendid disregard of external values in this juxtaposition and it was a summing up of the best part of the pre-Raphaelite attitude to life.

VI

ON the top floor of the blue staircase was a bedroom where Nanny and our baby sister slept and next to it the maids' bedroom into which I never penetrated in all the years I stayed at Rottingdean. There was a complete taboo on their door and my brother and I who were only too ready to go anywhere when we weren't wanted never once dared to attempt the adventure. This same taboo was on the kitchen which we never dreamed of visiting without an invitation, whether it was the temporary abode of Mr. and Mrs. Mounter, or Mrs. Snudden from the village, or a London cook who was brought down for the holidays. It was unexpected to find a basement kitchen of the worst period of Victorian civilization in a whitewashed cottage. Both kitchen and scullery were well below the ground-level and lighted by windows which looked out, the one into an area some three feet wide, the other on to the brick steps by which the tradesmen came down with their parcels. There was no through ventilation except what came through a couple of iron gratings in the brick path behind the house and the larder was tucked away near one of them. In later years a passage was made under the corner of the hall to join the kitchen to the boot and knife and furnace establishment in the brown-staircase house, but in early days the kitchen was a dark cellar, very different from the large airy ground-floor kitchen of my grandparents' house in London. However, maids were used to troglodyte conditions and in winter it was at least deliciously warm with a huge fire in the little room. In summer they opened the window, hung up quantities of fly-papers and took things as they came.

When we went down to the beach in the morning the kitchen often provided us with slices of dripping cake and a friendly cook waved good-bye from the window as the nursery cavalcade set out. The procession beachwards used to begin about ten o'clock on weekday mornings in August and September—on Sundays Nanny would not allow us to go within sight of the sea—with perambulators coming majestically out of all the houses where there were nurseries. First came our perambulator pushed by Nanny in her summer uniform of stiff white piqué and severe straw hat (for even Nannies wore boaters in the 'nineties), containing my baby sister, my brother with his legs dangling over the side, two wooden spades, two tin pails, and all the family bathing dresses and towels. I walked beside them with a green sixpenny shrimping net in which nothing was ever caught and the shilling for buns tightly clasped in my hand. At the corner of the green we were joined by the contingent of visiting grandchildren from The Dene, Didi, Lorna, Margot who was christened Pamela Margaret but called herself Perambulator Margaret, and Oliver. The other brother and sister came later and never really belonged to those days. Our Nanny and the Baldwins' head nurse were firm friends and Edie, the pale-eyed, fair-haired nursery maid, was allowed to be a hanger-on at their gossipings. So the perambulators and nurses and children swept down the village street in a solid phalanx, moving aside for nothing less than the half-past-ten bus as it wandered round the village collecting passengers for Brighton.

All down the street were friends to greet. Mrs. Ridsdale bearing down on us like a galleon, Mr. Ridsdale with his velvet coat, Arthur Ridsdale the doctor, off on his horse to some outlying farm. Then Julian Ridsdale and Aurelian Ridsdale, with Uncle Phil and our cousin Ambrose Poynter, the last two down for a week-end, all wondering what to do and very ready to tease the nursery party for want of better employment. Aurelian and my grandmother had lately had a friendly dispute over a matter of a few pounds which each insisted was due to the other from some committee, and Aurelian had cut the knot by putting it into three Post Office Savings Bank accounts for myself and my brother and sister. It was the first time the nursery had had a banking account and I, being over seven, had the unfair advantage of being able to withdraw my wealth personally. Aurelian was the justest as he was the most generous and upright of men. There was always considerable confusion in my mind about his name because the Ridsdales had brought pieces of cornelian back from Egypt and I didn't see why one name should be used rather than the other. Julian though, with his easy lazy banter, was perhaps the nursery favourite.

Three Houses

Then Mr. Green would come by, or Miss Mabel Green whose cheerful habit of countenance made Didi Baldwin call her 'Miss Smileyface' and be horribly scolded by her nurse for impertinence, or Miss Bates who always walked solitary with a black poodle. As we passed by the shingle-covered road that led to Hilder the butcher's house and shop, the noise of home-killed South Down mutton might come bleatingly and bellowingly to our ears. Then there might be the vicar whose Adam's apple surpassed in size that of all other clergymen, or his successor who shocked the nursery, always staunch Conservatives, by wearing an open collar and white tie instead of the conventional dog-collar. Then from various lodgings in the village other children joined the beach party. All Herbert Trench's boys and girls with their friend Peggy Middleton who were lodged during the holidays in some of the buildings of St. Aubyn's school and had the school gymnasium as their most enviable playground. Gillie and Chrissie whose father was, we understood, a very glorified kind of policeman. Their elder brother and sister Charlie and Julia—poor Charlie who had a banjo and used to play 'When Father laid the carpet on the stairs' in the Mermaid on a summer afternoon, with all my family and The Dene and Hillside applauding. He was at odds with life for many years. Then his name shone at Gallipoli, but he aged too soon and died in another land, so far from the youngster who sang at Rottingdean.

All the summers run into one as the young shadows of so many friends come to join us. Viola and Una Taylor talking French with their mother, which seemed a little suspicious to our less cosmopolitan nursery, Viola adoring my little brother and giving me a set of Miss Edgeworth's *Early Lessons*, a very early edition with tiny steel engravings pasted in as vignettes for chapter headings; Molly Stanford, dark and long-legged, from her father's school. There were two boys' schools at Rottingdean, St. Aubyn's in the village, owned by Mr. Stanford, and a newer school out beyond the village on the road to Woodendean kept then by a Mr. Mason. The village's estimation of the two schools was shown in those days by the one being known as 'Mr. Stanford's' and the other simply as 'Mason's'. Oliver Baldwin was to go to Mr. Stanford's school later, and when Didi Baldwin grew up her little boy was to go there too. Mr. Stanford was related to our beloved 'Aunt Madeline', Mrs. Percy Wyndham, and so had some of the blood of Lord Edward Fitzgerald and the enchanting Pamela, and more than one Fitzgerald descendant was at his school.

If we were lucky Nanny might have to stop at the village Post Office and we could talk to Mrs. Champion and look covetously at the iron spades which were absolutely forbidden to us in case we cut off our toes. Mrs. Champion also sold buckets and shrimping nets and sandshoes and quantities of shell-ornamented boxes which I still think are among the most ravishing products of art. The *chef d'œuvre* of the Champion collection was a little mirror encrusted with coloured shells such as any mermaid might have been proud to own. It was so much admired by the fastidious Charles Ricketts that I had to get him one for his private collection.

Then came the baker's shop kept by our friend Mr. Stenning. He was undoubtedly the stoutest man ever made,

and rumour had it that he spent all his holidays at Dieppe—
an easy journey from Rottingdean which was only a few
miles from Newhaven—where his bulk, discreetly veiled in
a black alpaca jacket, was less noticed among the portly Gauls
than on his native beach. But I have never known a man
with such a noble conception of buns. His penny buns were
larger than the largest Bath Buns, fine upstanding voluptuous
creatures warm from the oven with a deep brown ambrosial
varnish on their outsides, heavy with currants and sultanas
and more spice-flavoured than any ordinary hot-cross bun.
We usually bought a shilling's worth—thirteen buns in
those spacious days—to take down to the beach for the
bathers after their encounter with the icy summer waters
of the Channel.

After this we might exchange a few pleasantries with
Mr. Shergold (mysteriously known to us as Shamrock),
who drove the village fly. My brother, seating himself one
day against orders on the back of the fly, was carried far
away into the distance, too frightened to jump off, and had
to walk miles back along the hot road. A little further on an
archway on the right led under some cottages to Rottingdean's indubitable slum called Golden Square, where several
families lived in great squalor within a stone's throw of the
open downs. Mr. Murphy, the head of one Irish family, was
blind of an eye, and was held up to us as an awful warning
because his trade was stone-breaking and he would not
wear glasses to protect his eyes and one day a splinter flew
into his eye and he was blind to this day. Where exactly the
moral came in I don't know, as our opportunities of stone-
breaking were practically non-existent; but it impressed us

very much. One of his daughters, Annie, entered my mother's service in an ill-omened hour as between maid, and inaugurated her service by leaving an oil lamp turned up so high that the bedroom which it was to have warmed was knee deep in soot before my mother was alarmed by the smell and rushed upstairs. Then we might have to stop at Mrs. Mockford's little shop to order fruit for North End House and buy a penny bar of Fry's chocolate cream.

The approach to the beach was down a cutting in the chalk cliff between grass banks, where there was a hand winch to wind the fishing boats well above the high-tide mark in stormy weather. Each perambulator had to be got down separately by two Nannies, the one behind straining on the handle to act as brake, the one in front walking backwards holding on to the folded hood in case the whole machine got out of control and plunged down the steep descent. Not till all three perambulators, one of ours and two from The Dene, were safely stowed on a little bit of level ground at the bottom were the younger children allowed to get out and stagger across the shingle to the place which the senior Nanny had chosen for the morning's camp. Here rugs were spread and the most tremendous amount of dressing took place before we were allowed to paddle. In those days no one had thought of anything better than heavy blue serge for little girls to wear at the sea. Our cuffs were unbuttoned and turned up to the elbows, our skirts were gathered into a handful behind and twisted like a rope and rammed into our voluminous serge knickerbockers, which must have given us a curiously bunchy look, and we were allowed to take our shoes and stockings off and put sand-

shoes on. Then the legs of our knickerbockers were rolled
up as high as they would go and with awful warnings against
getting wet we were let loose with spades and buckets. What
happened to the younger children I don't remember.
Certainly the Nannies wouldn't have trusted them to us and
equally they would never have spoilt their morning's chat
—'talking about Him and Her' we used to call it—by
escorting their young charges to the water. I can only
suppose that the babies played with pebbles or banged their
pails on the stones for sheer joy of the noise till some one
stopped them.

If it was a lucky morning the tide was low so that we
could dig in the wet sand and explore the rocks, and just
on the turn so that we could bathe later on when the grown-
ups came down; a great host of parents and friends and
relations accompanied by the third contingent of cousins
in perambulators from The Elms. They could not come
earlier because they had a governess as well as a nurse and
they are harder to get started.

And now everything was in train for bathing. That
science had made but little progress since the days of Leech's
drawings of pretty ladies coming out of the canvas hoods of
bathing machines and horrible old bathing women with
bonnets, apparently walking about in the sea all fully dressed.
On the beach above high-water mark was a row of bathing
machines, little houses with pointed roofs and a door at each
end with a flight of steps to let down. When the tide was
right for bathing the boatmen used to push them down the
shingly slope to the water's edge and it was our great am-
bition to get into the machines and go down to the sea in

triumph. Of all uncomfortable places for bathing Rottingdean was perhaps the worst. The sea there was of such
paralysing coldness that you could only dash in, swim
violently about, and dash out again. The beach was entirely
composed of shingle except at the lowest of tides when a little
sand appeared among the rocks. The chalk cliffs afflicted
one with blindness by their glare on sunny days and though
they sheltered one from the north wind when it happened
to blow, they were no protection against the more usual
south-west gale which flattened you against them and blew
what sand there was into your face. There were many days
when the sea was fringed with a line of seaweed and dirt
through which you had to wade to open water. When the
wind blew from the east, the late contents of your waste-
paper basket drifted ashore from the rubbish tip further up
the Channel. Yet in spite of all these drawbacks there was a
glamour about the beach at Rottingdean that no discomfort
could dispel.

I always shared a machine with Lily Ridsdale who could
brave the stormiest seas and had me under her charge.
Inside the little house it was deliciously snug. There was a
seat along each side and a little window with a wooden
shutter that one could pull across. I can still smell the damp
seaweedy smell and feel the wet sandy floor under my bare
feet. The machine was like a door into a different world.
You had gone up a ladder from a beach full of friends, with
boats and cliffs and everything safe; you emerged through
the further door upon a waste of waters which were already
lapping round the foot of your ladder. It needed some
courage to make the first strokes in that cold tossing sea,

but with Lily one was quite safe and could swim out to the
end of the pier and back. How one kept afloat at all in the
dresses one had to wear then I can't imagine. My grandmother had brought me a particularly fashionable one from
Paris. It was of heavy dark blue serge in two pieces. The
knickerbocker part was very baggy and buttoned just above
the knee; the tunic part had a very full skirt knee length,
puffed sleeves, a high neck and enormous collar or cape
embroidered with daisies. I don't know why I wasn't pulled
down by the sheer weight to a fishy death, but it was the thing
and one accepted it. On the shore my mother would sit,
watch in hand, anxiously counting the minutes, and the
moment our time was up she waved a white handkerchief
and we had to come in.

And now came the most exciting part of the morning.
Far above us on the cliff was a capstan from which long wire
ropes, over which everybody tripped, hung down to the
beach. A hook at the end of this rope was attached to the
bathing machine and a donkey began to walk round and
round the capstan hauling us up. It was delirious joy to
feel the little house beginning to move, to hear first the
swish of the waves against the side and then the scrunch of
wheels on shingle as the donkey pursued his round and we
went higher and higher up the beach. Then we were un-
hooked and a small, damp, dishevelled, sandy figure pre-
cipitated herself down the steps with her bundle. Those
serge bathing dresses were beyond human power to wring
out unaided and a very horny-handed old boatman, or sometimes Mr. Trunky Thomas himself, who owned the machines,
if he happened to be doing nothing particular on the beach

at the moment, used to twist them into ropes and hang them out to dry. Then there were warm buns to eat while Nanny dried and brushed my hair.

By this time a little crowd was collecting on the pier and if my brother and I could find a suitable escort (for we were never allowed to do anything alone, possibly with reason), we had permission to join it. An uncle, or good-natured Julian Ridsdale, would volunteer to look after us and off we would go to see the arrival of the Daddy Long-legs. This was the most preposterous machine which came on railway lines through the sea from Brighton every day. Huge blocks of concrete had been laid in the sea with lines on them and along these rolled a kind of elevated platform with four immensely long legs ending in great boxes with wheels inside them. It was more like a vision of the Martians than anything you ought to see at a peaceful seaside village. We were never allowed to go in it, partly because no grown-up thought it amusing enough to go with us and partly because it had a habit of sticking somewhere opposite the ventilating shaft of the Brighton main sewer and not being moved till nightfall. When it had discharged its passengers at the pier it took on a fresh load and stalked back again to Brighton leaving us in gaping admiration.

Now the voices of the Nannies were heard summoning us to be packed up. The babies were stowed into their perambulators, the perambulators were pulled and pushed up the steep ascent and the phalanx returned up the village street. As we approached North End House we saw Ernest, the garden boy, come out with a bucket of water and a syringe. These were the well-known preparations for the peculiar Rottingdean methods of window-cleaning. It was rather disconcerting if you were sitting in the drawing-room window seat to have a syringe full of water suddenly battering the panes. Ernest and the housemaid frequently had 'words' on the subject of squirting the windows before she had got them properly shut. We should have loved to help, but Nanny wouldn't hear of it, so we had to follow her in.

The bathing things were spread to dry on the warm brick path or on the sweetbriar hedge. The house and garden were very still under the noontide sun and the scent of the sweetbriar was in the air. A cock crowed from the stable-yard next door and a sheep bell sounded somewhere up on Windmill Hill. My baby sister was left asleep in the perambulator in the garden while my brother and I were sent upstairs to rest. We took off our beach things, pulled the white honeycomb counterpanes off our beds and lay down. Then Nanny came up and drew the curtains. The room was luminous with sunlight penetrating the blue Morris chintz and I could quite well see my angel at the foot of my bed pulling away the curtain of darkness to let in the light, till at last I fell asleep.